10

WOMEN
WHO
WERE
SPIRITUAL
MOTHERS

——✕——

**Dayspring
MacLeod**

CHRISTIAN
FOCUS

Copyright © Dayspring MacLeod 2023

paperback ISBN 978-1-5271-0972-8
ebook ISBN 978-1-5271-1024-3

10 9 8 7 6 5 4 3 2 1

Published in 2023 by
Christian Focus Publications, Ltd.
Geanies House, Fearn,
Ross-shire, IV20 1TW, Scotland.
www.christianfocus.com

Cover design by Pete Barnsley

Printed and bound by
Bell & Bain, Glasgow

MIX
Paper | Supporting
responsible forestry
FSC® C007785

This is a surprising book. It is not afraid to tread in difficult places. It is not just the stories of inspiring women; it challenges readers with the strength of the Scriptures. That is why it is able to offer comfort.

Kirsten Birkett
Author of *Imperfect Reflections*

Dayspring has done it again! This new volume about ten more interesting women and their roles as mothers—some living centuries ago, and some contemporary, is a great read. It was both profitable and convicting to study well known women in a new way and to be introduced to the stories of mothers not previously known. As an author on the topic of gratitude, I appreciate how gratitude comes up over and over again in Dayspring's careful reflections on what is key in our walk with the Lord. This book encouraged me to seek to be be a valiant woman who pours into the life of others to God's glory.

Mary K. Mohler
Director, Seminary Wives Institute
Author, *Growing in Gratitude*

This is a book about motherhood in the widest possible meaning of the word. Dayspring MacLeod is a mother of three and her story is woven into the book alongside the stories of ten other women from different parts of the world and times in history. The tapestry the author weaves portrays the reality of both physical motherhood and spiritual motherhood: the joys, the aching pains, hopes realised, deferred or denied. All of them lead to the comforting yet appallingly difficult place where we are given what it takes to hand all to our Heavenly Father, praying, 'Your will be done.'

Some of the mothers in the book bore no children but reared those of others, one prayed for decades before her wayward son was converted and for another mothering is mentoring many others as well as her own. Being married to an internationally known preacher has never been easy and bringing up ministry children brings its own peculiar challenges. And imagine the family dynamic when prison, new baby, autism and conversion all feature in one family's life experience. It is little wonder that mothers need mothering more often that we care to admit and the book provides us with a fine example of just that. A godly stepmother is found in the pages of the book – and she is also found in the history of the English monarchy. American history provides Dayspring with the story of a mother who lived at the time of the Civil War. Her mothering was done in the most difficult of circumstances. The last woman in the book is right up to date and comes with the assurance that 'we can fail BIG, but never bigger than God's love for us.'

The background to this book's tapestry is the Bible and Dayspring MacLeod weaves what God's Word has to say into each subject tackled.

This is not a book for the faint-hearted but neither is motherhood in any of its forms. Each chapter ends with focusing the reader's mind of some relevant Bible verses then posing a few searching questions. It is not a book to be read right through in one sitting. Time spent on this serious study of motherhood will bear fruit in families and church families. To God be the glory!

Irene Howat
Award-winning author

Contents

To Mom: not just a Proverbs 31 woman, but a 1 Corinthians 13 woman. She speaks to us of Christ all the time, but she shows us Christ with that love that bears all things, believes all things, hopes all things, endures all things.

Introduction

Welcome to you readers who are biological mothers in need of some inspiration to cope with exhausting toddlers, precocious kids and difficult teenagers. Welcome to you who are battling infertility and feel the tears will never stop, and the emptiness will never end. Welcome to you who are single and almost didn't pick up this book because you don't feel the word *mother* will ever belong to you; perhaps you aren't sure you even want it to. To those who feel they are failing so hard that they don't deserve the word *mum*. To those who feel forgotten by God. To those who don't feel up to pouring spiritual life into someone else's cup. I am right here with you.

I want to speak to each of you – anxious, hopeful, weary, ready, wherever you are in life – as valiant women. To explain why, I'm going to summarise teaching by Rabbi Cosmo Panzetta, a Messianic pastor serving in Arizona.[1]

---

1. You can listen to the full sermon here: https://www.youtube.com/watch?v=aURB0zfMK7M, House of New Beginnings, 'Eishet Chayil: The Valiant Woman.' Shabbat LIVE May 8, 2021, Rabbi Cosmo Panzetta. Teaching begins 23 minutes into video.

We are all aware of the Proverbs 31 woman, often called 'an excellent woman', 'a virtuous woman', 'a noble woman', 'a capable woman'. But the phrase actually used in the Hebrew, *eishet chayil*, means a woman of strength – of valour. 'A valiant woman!' There's a difference between saying someone's capable and someone's valiant. Think of soldiers. A capable soldier won't lose the battle for you, but a valiant soldier sacrificially leads you to victory.

We're used to employing soft, tame words for biblical women. This woman is heroic, one who gives her life to defend what she loves. There's only one specific woman in Scripture of whom the phrase *eishet chayil* is used, and we find this in Ruth 3:11. Boaz tells Ruth, 'Everyone in town knows that you are a valiant woman.' The only woman in all of Scripture who gets this designation, at the time, was not a wife, but a widow. She was not a mother. She wasn't even Jewish. She wasn't wealthy like the Valiant Woman of Proverbs 31; she was gleaning the edges of a field, the leftovers. She was taking the little she had and making a life of it.

If you're not a wife, not a mother, you can still be a Valiant Woman. None of those things are necessary to be a woman of valour. But there are three character traits that define this woman.

1. The Valiant Woman gives her life away. We live in a society that says 'you've got to take care of yourself,' but there's a selflessness in Ruth. Similarly, the Proverbs 31 woman uses her wealth for the benefit of others. Being a Valiant Woman is not based on your status, but your character.

2. The Valiant Woman is faithful with her gifts, abilities and resources. One thing that all of us are able to do is to love faithfully. It's a characteristic that overflows from the Lord: His love, His kindness and loyalty. He is overflowing in love, and we are to be too.

3. The Valiant Woman fears the Lord. Ruth made a perm-anent break with her past, and she made a permanent commitment to the Lord. Imagine that in the circumstances! She had seen Naomi lose everything; she had lost her own husband. Despite all the tragedy, she had come to know this God through Naomi. She places her trust in Him. Every other quality in a Valiant Woman is an overflow from this essential trait of trusting the Lord.

A woman of valour is defined by selflessness, diligence, and godliness. These things will define your relationships: the kind of friend you'll be, aunt you'll be, godmother you'll be. In Jewish communities, we sing Proverbs 31 at the funeral of a mother. At your funeral, the only thing that matters is the legacy you leave: what you poured into others.

Think of a mother in the Bible, and who comes to your mind? For most people it is probably Mary, the mother of Jesus. We know that Mary had an upstanding character, because God chose her for a unique purpose and called her 'blessed above all women'. But what was Mary like as a mother?

Mary no doubt taught little Yeshua His numbers and letters and table manners. But what we actually see in the

Scripture is not her teaching her son, but *learning* from Him, and teaching others to learn from Him.

In Luke 2, following her son's birth with its many signs, Mary *took these things and pondered them in her heart.* The star, the shepherds, the stable, the magi: all were things she meditated on and learned from.

When Jesus disappeared in the Temple during a family holiday, Mary gave Him a telling off, but she also learned more about who He was. 'Did you not know I must be about my Father's business?', He asked, assuming she already understood more than she did. No doubt the writers of the Gospels heard this story from Mary herself, as she looked back in wonder that she had as yet realised so little!

At the wedding in Cana, Mary pushed her child to fulfil His purpose, but the instruction she gave was not to Him, but to the servants: 'Whatever he tells you to do, do it.' By now she had learned that this son was one who bore authority and wisdom beyond her.

Throughout Jesus' life, Mary is never far behind. She goes to Him as He ministers to crowds, and asks to see Him; Jesus responds, 'Who is my mother and who are my brothers? He who hears my word, and does it.' This places the crowds themselves in a position of intimacy with Him, but it also teaches Mary that her primary relationship to Jesus is not the celebrity 'mother of God', but a subject of the King.

When He goes to the cross, she follows, despite the unbearable pain of watching Him die, and enters into a new relationship as mother to the apostle John, presumably as Jesus' brothers were not yet believers and therefore unable to pastor her spiritually. That spiritual family has now taken precedence over the earthly, transient family. She learns faithfulness even beyond Jesus' death, as she becomes a quiet but integral part of the early Church. Mary's heart remains teachable; and she remains a disciple of her son, of her Saviour, for her entire life.

Jesus had the best of all mothers, and yet He out-mothers her. He is the eternal God who gathers His people under His wings like a mother hen.[2] He is the One who bore, and will carry, His beloved children even into old age.[3] Jesus is the ultimate nurturer. And His Spirit is the One who, when we are too confused and weary and sad even to know what to ask Him for, petitions the Father on our behalf![4]

In a book about mothers, it is impossible not to think of my own: a woman who loves the Word of God, a trusted counsellor to anyone in trouble, sacrificial in caring and listening, a loving and patient nurturer, as beautiful and warm inside as outside. I think too of many 'mothers in Israel'[5] – those who have taken me under their wing, especially after I moved countries, who provided me with compassion and comfort and a true sense of Jesus' love in the absence of my own mother.

When I think of my relationship with my own children – whether the little ones who live in my home, or the spiritual

---

2. Matthew 23:3.

3. Isaiah 46:4.

4. Romans 8:26.

5. This phrase is used in the Bible of the judge Deborah, who is known for her leadership qualities rather than her motherhood! There is an interesting article about 'Mothers in Israel' at https://meetjesusatuni.com/2010/12/01/what-is-a-mother-in-israel/

'children' I have befriended or mentored – I see mostly my failures. My lack of discipline, patience, consistency, faithfulness, grace. I so often see, through outward eyes as it were, how I treat others and I think, *that is not how my Lord deals with me.* Surely the Lord looks compassionately on my weakness, limitations and forgetfulness; how I pray that, through writing this book, He will make my heart much more like His own. And I pray that for you too, dear sister.

1. A Mother who is Happy

Lisa Harper

Lisa Harper is an American writer and Christian speaker who recently published a book called *The Sacrament of Happy*. The amazing thing is that she has every reason not to be happy. In her early life, Lisa was traumatised by her parents' ugly divorce. Her father was a changeable man with a temper. In late childhood, she was molested by multiple men connected with her family. A child psychologist once told her mother, 'Lisa is either the most happy, well-adjusted child I've ever met in my life, or she is in deep emotional pain' – and her mother went around boasting to everyone that Lisa was incredibly happy and well-adjusted![1] These terrible experiences marred the Baptist upbringing Lisa received, and yet she remained with the Lord and sought to glorify Him with her life. Eventually, the strain of serving while still struggling to process all that trauma stopped her in her tracks, and she had a panic attack while leading a women's Bible study.

---

1. Lisa Harper, *The Sacrament of Happy: What a Smiling God Brings to a Wounded World*, (B&H Publishing Group: Nashville, 2017), p. 8.

... I got into my car, called a therapist, and made the first appointment of what turned into almost a decade of digging. When you've become a master faker like I had, the truth gets buried pretty deep. While I believe that all of life's answers can be found in God's Word, I've realized I often need the help of those wiser than me to find them and apply them to the most wounded places of my heart. Sometimes we need triage before we can get back up and fight the good fight. Before we can actually participate in the fulness of joy instead of just pretending we're happy.[2]

Therapy eventually helped Lisa to move on with her life, and, as she passed child-bearing age, she started to seek the Lord as to whether she might adopt a child. She asked three Christian friends to pray for her in that decision. Two were willing to do so and encouraged her, but the third felt Lisa was still too damaged from her past and should settle for another dog. It was another five years before Lisa felt 'whole' enough to pursue adoption – and she knew she wanted a child who wouldn't have much of a chance at being chosen by a regular two-parent family. After two heartbreaking failed attempts to adopt, Lisa met Missy, an HIV-positive toddler with a grocery list of further medical problems, and fell in love with her, so much so that she decided she would move to Haiti to be with her if that was the only route open. In her book, Lisa talks about the secret to her overwhelming happiness:

Because I'm fifty-three and single, I often teasingly say, 'My husband is lost and won't stop to ask for directions.' But the truth of the matter is that the main reason I'm single is

2.   Ibid, p.5.

because I was very broken and foolish in my twenties and thirties. Most of the men I was attracted to were abusive in some way – largely because of childhood trauma and sexual abuse, destructive personal relationships were my default setting for decades – so God protected me from them. And the few kind, Christian men I dated for any length of time, God protected from me because I was such a romantic train wreck. It took me a really long time to recognize and admit I needed deep emotional healing, and by that time not only had I squandered the typical matrimony years of young adulthood, but I'd almost missed the biological window of motherhood ... I do believe there are consequences to sin, and the consequence of my relational toxicity was that I never trusted a man enough to marry him and never got to experience the miracle of pregnancy. So the fact that God not only withheld His anger over my fear and foolishness but also restored to me the years I'd allowed 'locusts' to devour (Joel 2:25) by allowing me to become Missy's mom when I was fifty years old has left me intoxicated with gratitude.[3]

* * *

For his anger is but for a moment, and his favour is for a lifetime. Weeping may tarry for the night, but joy comes with the morning (Psalm 30:5).

I remember a couple of years ago, when I had only two children and they were both toddlers, saying to a friend, 'I love being a mum, but I don't love being a stay-at-home mom.' That might have been a fair comment – we're not all cut out to live the same lifestyle – but I'm not sure it was quite true. I'm not sure I loved being a mum at all.

---

3.   Ibid, pp. 136-137.

When I was a child we had a grumpy, bedraggled-looking poodle mix called Lady. Lady had two litters of six puppies each, and I remember the sight of her, irritable and sore, trying to slink away from her offspring even as they tried to feed from her, dragging them along on their stumbling little paws and ignoring their whines. *Lady's a bad mother*, I remember thinking. *She just wants to get away from her puppies all the time. She doesn't even love them!*

Fast-forward twenty years, and there I was daily trying to carve out even minutes away from my own children. Well, it didn't start out that way. At one time that attitude was unimaginable.

Happiness through Childlessness

I could never go into the infertility ward of the Edinburgh Royal Infirmary without bursting into tears at some point, and from that moment on I would be basically unable to say anything intelligible. What made it worse is that the infertility unit was actually connected to the delivery unit, which meant that you would see huge-bellied mothers about to meet their new baby everywhere you looked, and then you would go into a doctor's office to hear about a terrifying range of needles you would be expected to employ on your own for weeks to have even a chance of a pregnancy. It was a particularly dark time, making the decision whether IVF was for us, and eventually I prayed to the Lord that although I didn't want to go through with it, I had to leave this decision in His hands: if we didn't conceive naturally by a certain date, after a planned holiday, we would go ahead. A number of miracles later, we found out we were pregnant – the day before I was to call the clinic and set up the treatment.

I know a great many women who have experienced infertility. Some have gone on to have children, some also under miraculous circumstances. Some have not, but have gone on faithfully loving and serving the Lord anyway. Some have had miscarriages or infant loss. I also know many who would love to be mothers but have never had a long-term relationship, much less met the man they wanted to raise a family with.

In the years we endured our struggle, the least helpful thing people said to me was, 'Don't worry, it'll happen. You just have to relax.' Because, of course, they didn't know that. They didn't know the plan God had for our lives. And we don't need to give infertile (or single, or grieving) women false hope – because we have true hope.

Last Christmas, it suddenly stuck me that infertility in the Bible is always presented as an opportunity for God to do something wonderful. Every single time. All the women of Israel we see struggling to conceive, and crying out – Sarah, Rebekah, Hannah, Rachel, Elisabeth – went on to have children who heralded great changes in God's master plan. Why? Because in showing that He could intervene in doing what seemed impossible for these women, and accomplishing great things through them, He foreshadowed that He would do the actual impossible, and accomplish the

> *Infertility in the Bible is always presented as an opportunity for God to do something wonderful. Every single time.*

greatest of all things. A virgin would conceive, and bring forth a Son, and He would be called Immanuel. God walking among us; God in human skin. The difficulty of birth from infertility pointed to the miracle of divine birth from virginity.

Not every woman who experiences childlessness will have this kind of miracle. Very often, God chooses to do a 'new thing' when we would prefer our own desire, our own solution. But as 'God among us' was a miracle, so 'God through us' is as well. What the Almighty can accomplish through a woman who offers Him her broken heart has no bounds.

> *As 'God among us' was a miracle, so 'God through us' is as well. What the Almighty can accomplish through a woman who offers Him her broken heart has no bounds.*

Anna had been a widow for decades and it was not until her eighties that God allowed her both to hold and to prophesy over His infant Son. Lydia had no family mentioned but she was a beloved mother to an emerging church. Esther saved all the Jews of an empire. Mary of Magdala was lonely and demon-possessed but became one of Jesus' first disciples. Ruth, as we showed earlier, was a woman of valour. So often, God gives us something, whether a task or a blessing, much bigger than anything we would have imagined for ourselves.

Okay, I'm going to go there. Deep breath.

'Sing, O barren one, who did not bear; break forth into singing and cry aloud, you who have not been in labour! For the children of the desolate one will be more than the children

of her who is married,' says the LORD. 'Enlarge the place of your tent, and let the curtains of your habitations be stretched out; do not hold back; lengthen your cords and strengthen your stakes. For you will spread abroad to the right and to the left, and your offspring will possess the nations and your people the desolate cities.

'Fear not, for you will not be ashamed; be not confounded, for you will not be disgraced; for you will forget the shame of your youth, and the reproach of your widowhood you will remember no more. For your Maker is your husband, the LORD of Hosts is his name ... For the LORD has called you like a wife deserted and grieved in spirit, like a wife of youth when she is cast off ... for a brief moment I deserted you, but with great compassion I will gather you.'[4]

I have to say these are, straight-up, some of the most offensive verses in the entire Bible. You didn't get the thing you wanted most in all your life? It's all good! Sing a song! *Forget about it!* If this was the message from a person in your life, you'd call them heartless – after all, they don't have the power to bring joy out of despair. But because He does, let's look at the heart of God.

The book of Isaiah is all about hope when hope is gone. God is speaking here not just to barren women but to a nation that was now in captivity. The land itself was barren, the homes smouldering ruins. There was emptiness, yet He could see the time coming when the tents of Israel would be bursting with the peoples of the world, all because of the coming Messiah who would be the fruit of the union between

---

4.   Isaiah 54:1-7.

God and His people. We have seen some of that prophecy fulfilled already, and I believe we will see new levels of it in ages to come. What God's Word says is trustworthy. It comes to pass, miracles and all.

God is also saying that those who feel empty, who feel rejected, who feel desolate and humiliated and like failures, are the very ones who are going to be filled and glorified and, well, happy. Those who are trusting in the Lord through their very disappointment, their heartbreak – they

> *God is also saying that those who feel empty, who feel rejected, who feel desolate and humiliated and like failures, are the very ones who are going to be filled and glorified and, well, happy.*

shouldn't take these things as the evidence of their rejection by the Lord. Instead, they should rejoice as if they've already received the fulfilment of their longing, and should prepare their place to receive abundance – because, as surely as God brought His people safe through captivity and planted them back in their land, He can fill you too.

Keep your eyes open. Not just for what you expect Him to do, but for whatever He might do! It may not be that you will have children in the way you expect, but whatever His plan is, for the woman who seeks and loves Him, it is to fill her up completely. It might be through doing His work. It might be through adoption. It might be through mentoring younger Christians. It might be through a career that becomes a calling. It might be through following a mother-in-law to her hometown, or elevation to the monarchy in turbulent times, or showing generosity to those in need. But one thing is sure: if it is going to truly fill us to bursting, it HAS to mean a filling of Jesus and His Spirit. 'I have come to give life, and give it abundantly,' Jesus says. And another way to read that? He is the only way to find abundant life. Let me explain.

Reasons to be Grateful

I know some of you, who have not had biological children, were probably seething at my description of my ingratitude and impatience with my own babies. I know that feeling: a pregnant friend would complain to me about her nausea or something, and I would think *you are complaining to the wrong person.* Remember, these are the children I had begged God for, a desire of my heart that I felt would never come. And here is the hard truth of it.

Without having your greatest desires submitted to Christ and shaped by Christ, receiving them is utterly unfulfilling. Unless gratitude to Christ, recognising that even the hard parts are part of His blessing, is a habit of your heart, then all these gifts will lose their shine.

Without having your greatest desires submitted to Christ and shaped by Christ, receiving them is utterly unfulfilling.

Look at examples from your own life and you'll know it to be true. You were desperate to get that job, but now you hate Monday mornings. You waited months for him to propose, but there are days you still feel alone. You were so excited to move to the new flat, but now you're homesick for your old town. You were so glad about that pay rise, but now you want to upgrade your car and the money's short again.

So it is for motherhood: you dreamed of running your fingers through their little curls, but now if you hear '*Muuuu-uuuum*' one more time you're going to charge into their bedroom with a tantrum of your own!

Without a conscious willingness toward gratitude, nothing of worldly value, even relationships, will ever satisfy you. Like a child asking for a new toy the week after the Christmas bonanza, you will always want something else out of your grasp. So how do you foster gratitude?

I'm going to tell you what worked for me. Thankfully, my selfishness and irritability wasn't the end of the story for my relationship with my children. We haven't got to the end yet, because God is still working on my heart. But there was, at least, a turn in direction. And it's a surprise twist.

The turn my life took was repentance. Gut-wrenching, open-eyed repentance about deep-seated attitudes in my own heart. I'll give you an example. When I called my pastor's wife one day crying because I could see how harsh I was being to my own child, she said, 'I never knew I was an angry person until I had children.' What I heard in that exchange was, 'Children just make everyone angry sometimes, even mellow people.' What I finally understood, several years on after the Lord intervened, was this: I have an anger problem. It was a latent area that I didn't realise was even in my heart, but there it was. I get unjustly angry. I have murder in my heart – murder of my own children. My babies, just by acting like babies do, finally showed up what was underneath the surface.

Now you'll be wondering where the gratitude comes in. Here it comes. *Thank you, Lord, for showing me this sinful attitude, because now I am asking you to help me defeat this sin.*

The gratitude is that Christ paid for all my selfishness, all my rage-filled hissing at being woken in the night, and somehow each day still chooses me to pour into their little hearts not only love, but also joy and godliness.

The gratitude is being able to see them as gifts, not as burdens, because when I asked God for the ability actually to enjoy my children instead of slogging on in my duty, He answered by changing my heart toward them.

The gratitude is knowing that the Lord is so much more tender toward my children – and toward me – than I ever am, even at my best, and that He will keep on transforming me to reflect His character, by and by.

Lisa quotes Randy Alcorn: 'With gratitude, there's happiness; without it, there's unhappiness. Every time.'[5]

I don't know what you have to repent of. I spent many years, even those exhausted and angry years, feeling like a super-good person and excellent Christian. Look how dutiful I was! How I always served myself last! How worn out my clothes and my eyes were! But beneath it, I was trying to hold myself together. May I never go back to that place.

Are you a complainer? Do you pretend everything's good when you're despairing over a secret vice? Do you look down on other Christians, much less the super sinful people outside your particular denomination? Do you make sure you're comfortable

---

5.   Harper, p.140.

and pampered before you give any of your money to the church or to others? Do you pine over what you don't have? Are there things in your life you simply don't want to surrender?

In my experience, gratitude begins with repentance. That's how far I've come in the story. But to go on, and Lisa makes this point in her book, solidify your gratitude by feeding it.

> Frankly, if we've put our hope in Jesus Christ, our thought life is under the authority of the Holy Spirit. That doesn't mean every single thing that sails through that space between our ears will be sacred, but we don't have to be controlled by pessimism, cynicism, or fear. As Martin Luther brilliantly observed, 'You can't stop the birds from flying over your head, but you can keep them from making a nest in your hair.'[6]

In my experience, gratitude begins with repentance.

Basically, the thoughts and feelings we dwell on go a long way toward determining our moods and attitudes. When I spend all my time thinking about how exhausted, martyred, homesick and *cough cough* *noble* I am as a mother, I feel ever more despairing, lonely, even hopeless. When I make a conscious decision to delight in Jesus, praise Him, ask Him for help, and walk in His presence, the burden lifts, and I feel very, very happy and satisfied in Him. I don't really know how else to put it: as an old Sunday School song says, *happiness is the Lord.*

So how do you give Him fulfilling and happy worship? Well, give thanks for all the good things in your life, sure. But give thanks when things are hard too. As nobody's favourite

---

6   Ibid, p.111.

verse says, 'Give thanks in all circumstances.'[7] Give thanks for the character God is forming in you. Give thanks that you're not alone. Give thanks that God is good, even when life is hard.

There is happiness in the Christian life. You don't have to feel it all the time. But know that, no matter what has happened to you, a life centred in Jesus will find joy – and *enjoyment* – again. Not joy with a sense of dread in the background. Not just joy amidst the tears. *Joy* joy. Abundant, overflowing joy! We open ourselves up to it with repentance. We feed it with giving thanks in all circumstances. How do we hold on to it in the midst of temptation or distraction or discouragement? We have Jesus' mind in ourselves.

Come with me.

Play to an Audience of One

There's a wonderful verse for keeping us motivated in living a humble and service-centred Christian life: 'Have this mind among yourselves, which is yours in Christ Jesus, who, though he was in the form of God, did not count equality with God a thing to be grasped (held onto), but emptied himself, by taking on the form of a servant ... he humbled himself by becoming obedient to the point of death, even death on a cross.'[8] I would suggest these verses also give us a hint toward living a happier Christian life.

How did Jesus stay humble, living as God in human form? How did He never once work for His own exultation, enjoy the flattery of people wanting to crown Him by force? How did He not get distracted by the power and earthly glory

7.   1 Thessalonians 5:16-18.

8.   Philippians 2:5-11.

of it? Right now, my last book is number 4 on Amazon's best-selling Religious Biographies categories and I feel like phoning up every publisher who ever rejected me just to do a mic drop. It's a fight to give God the glory even though I know that the start I made to that book in my own power, before God laid me low and then stepped in to work through me, was absolutely pitiful. I can categorically tell you that if the whole country was lauding me as the greatest teacher who ever lived, the Anointed One of God, I would absolutely take the compliment and consider my work done and accept all those tithes. Not go on to wash my students' feet and submit to a horrible death. So how did Jesus stay humble and happy, not grasping for power or recognition?

One, He was fixed on the needs of others and the will of His Father. Two, His divine nature was repelled by the ugliness of pride. But most of all, He was completely secure in who He was. He didn't need people to tell Him how fantastic that sermon was. He didn't need a promotion or award or bestseller list to feel validated. He didn't need to hear He was special. Being totally fulfilled by oneness with the Father – and listen, not the STATUS but the COMMUNITY of that oneness – He had no need of human approval. Instead He found rest in His Father's love ('This is my beloved Son, with whom I am well pleased')[9] and in withdrawing FROM those fickle crowds to enjoy His presence.

Why, then, are we told so often to praise and worship God in the Bible? Does He need built up, His triune ego stroked? Certainly not. He simply knows that in gratitude to Him we

---

9.   Matthew 3:17.

find our greatest happiness and fulfilment. Praise is nothing but rejoicing in God's goodness, and fellowshipping with Him. So, in Jesus, we know we can enjoy the belovedness of being His children, and we know that His comfort (and His pleasure in us) is sufficient for all our emotional needs. If we are looking for human approbation for our Christian work, then are we really doing it for Him?

Whatever you're doing, don't do it for people. People will forget to say thank you. They'll criticise your most heartfelt attempt to bless them. They'll fail to notice what you've done. They'll give someone else the credit. Your Father sees everything, and He longs to welcome you home with the words 'Good and Faithful Servant'. Bear in mind that Jesus' ministry was marked with only superficial human approval. Underneath all the hosannas, 'He came to his own, and his own people did not receive him.' But that did not dim His joy in the Father. He was playing to an audience of One.

Ever since I was little, I have struggled with a guilt and responsibility complex. It's called scrupulosity; you can look it up. I've had periods where it has tipped over into obsessive compulsive behaviour and it took me twenty minutes to leave the house for work every day because I had to start counting over and over again how many times I had checked the faucets or turned the key in the lock.

Your Father sees everything, and He longs to welcome you home with the words Good and Faithful Servant.

You know how sometimes a fact that you understand from the Bible suddenly jumps into technicolour, and it feels like it's real to you for the first time? Well, this Thanksgiving I was driving along to the shops, doing the normal rushed holiday errands, when I was struck by the thought *God doesn't see my sin*. I pulled into the shopping centre car park and bawled my eyes out because it occurred to me that God sees me as perfect and holy – so differently from how I see myself!

That doesn't mean that the Holy Spirit doesn't do His work of conviction and transformation. It doesn't mean that Jesus no longer has to intercede for me at His Father's right hand. But it does mean that when the Father looks at me, He looks through rose-coloured glasses: the colour of Jesus' redeeming blood. My sins, which were scarlet, are now like snow. My selfishness and irritability and ingratitude are cast away from me as far as east is from west. If you hate yourself, if you can't stop the guilt, if you will never be 'good enough' to profess faith publicly, if you are hopeless, if you can't find a motivation to praise or to serve, if you are ungrateful and unhappy, let that sink in.

God finds His pleasure, His happiness, in you. Where do you find yours?

How does Jesus Show Joy?

Lisa tells a story of taking Missy to get her quarterly HIV jabs: a process her daughter naturally hates and which always leads to panicked screaming. Instead of having Missy focus on the needle, Lisa gets her to look right in her eyes and focus on her mother's love. There's an obvious parallel with how we should live in times of confusion or discouragement: 'Wouldn't you know it, our happiness boils down to pretty much what I told

Missy a few weeks ago at the hospital: 'Focus on me, baby. Focus on me."[10]

We keep our eyes fixed on Jesus! So how does He show joy and happiness?

We don't see Jesus cracking a lot of jokes, unless you watch *The Chosen* – which I absolutely recommend, but unfortunately can't cite as Scripture. Where we do see Him, though, is at a wedding. You know the one. Either the bride and groom were poor or the guests were having a really good time, because they ran out of wine that day in Cana. Now, what was Jesus doing at that wedding? Was He prudishly shielding His eyes from the dancing? Did He mutter, 'About time they ran out – look at the state of Uncle Joachim'? We might have seen some Christians with that begrudging attitude, but not Jesus! He not only replenished the wine, He made it the best wine.

Here's a few things about wine in the Bible. One, it symbolises joy and abundance. It is often referred to in times of renewal and celebration, and not in a disparaging way either (while alcohol abuse is forbidden several times throughout both Testaments, using alcohol in a community setting carries no stigma). Jesus also talks about the ridiculousness of putting 'new wine' into old wineskins –

> *Now, what was Jesus doing at that wedding? Was He prudishly shielding His eyes from the dancing? Did He mutter, 'About time they ran out – look at the state of Uncle Joachim'?*

---

10. Harper, p. 61.

they'll burst and the wine and the skins are both ruined. You can't just shove the Holy Spirit into old religious practices or worldly attitudes. Our whole person needs to be made new too, ready to share out the good news. Finally, as well as symbolising joy and the Holy Spirit, there's a holiness to wine. It is a picture of Jesus' blood: something precious, set apart and beautiful, and provided as part of a holy Feast. And, even in the function of holiness, it doesn't lose the joy. That's still there in the background – because what is more joyful than knowing our sins are forgiven, that the Lord Jesus dwells in us? 'He who has no money, come, buy and eat! Come, buy wine and milk without money and without price.'[11]

Come to think of it, Jesus didn't provide just wine in His ministry. He went around spreading happiness. The happiness of physical healing. The happiness of freedom from an evil spirit. The happiness of tearing down religious walls that He never built in the first place. The happiness of a hated tax collector who suddenly found himself hosting the city's celebrity rabbi. The happiness of two sisters receiving their brother back from the dead. The happiness of Samaritans learning that, though they had rejected their Old Testament relationship with God, the Messiah had come to them anyway. People who opened themselves up to Jesus *found happy*.

And people who make others happy, people who give others hope, people who bring the biggest keg of the 'good stuff' to the party – those are happy people. And that's how we know that Jesus was absolutely brimming with joy.

---

11.   Isaiah 55:1.

Verses on Happiness and Gratitude

Then he said to them, 'Go your way. Eat the fat and drink sweet wine and send portions to anyone who has nothing ready, for this day is holy to our Lord. And do not be grieved, for the joy of the Lord is your strength' (Neh. 8:10).

This verse comes at a time when the people of Judah, having returned to Jerusalem after decades of captivity, hear the Law read out for the first time. They are filled with sorrow because of how they have broken God's Law – but it's the date of the Feast of Tabernacles, and instead of spending time stuck in guilt and repetitive repentance, God asks them instead to obey Him by rejoicing! Is it time for you to leave your old mistakes behind and praise Him as He has commanded? Can you be held up by the strength of His joy?

You make known to me the path of life; in your presence there is fulness of joy; at your right hand are pleasures forevermore (Ps. 16:11).

Sometimes it takes us a while of walking down life's path before we realise where it leads. that the best joy, the happiness like fine wine, the greatest pleasure that truly expands the human heart, is found in His presence. Do you trust that? Do you believe it? Then seek His presence, and walk your path even if it leads through the valley of the shadow of death. And make sure to notice happiness when it comes to you. Often the Lord speaks, assures or provides through the smallest of details. Look for them.

*The Lord your God is in your midst, a mighty one who will
save; he will rejoice over you with gladness; he will quiet you by
his love; he will exult over you with loud singing* (Zeph. 3:17).

What can I possibly add to this verse? Sit before the Lord to
feel your spirit quieting under His love. Listen for the sound
of His singing.

Questions

1. What are the specific attributes, stories or sayings of Jesus
   that make you feel delight in Him and ready to praise?
2. When do you struggle most with ingratitude? Are there
   sinful attitudes or behaviours that hamper your ability to
   have joy? How would it add to your happiness or freedom
   to know those sins are as far from you as east is from west?
3. What are you most grateful for in your life? What do you
   need to cultivate greater happiness?

> *Happiness is to know the Saviour*
> *Living a life within His favour*
> *Having a change in my behaviour*
> *Happiness is the Lord.*
>
> *True joy is mine*
> *No matter if the teardrops start*
> *I've found the answer*
> *It's Jesus in my heart!*
>
> *Happiness is to be forgiven*
> *Living a life that's worth the living*
> *Traveling the road that leads to heaven*
> *Happiness is the Lord!*
> – Ira F. Stanphill, Singspiration

2. A Spiritual Mother who Guided

Amy Carmichael

Amy Carmichael's life as a mother began unexpectedly. A single woman, she had already given up all the comforts and friends of home to join a missionary work in India. And she assumed she had found her calling, reaching the adults there with the good news of Jesus Christ, when she had an unexpected visitor. A little girl, a runaway, came to the mission station for refuge. Years later, she described her welcome there: 'Our precious Ammai was having her morning chota. When she saw me, the first thing she did was to put me on her lap and kiss me. I thought, 'My mother used to put me on her lap and kiss me – who is the person who kisses me like my mother?' From that day she became my mother.'[1]

The little girl had been sold by her family to become a temple prostitute. She was the first of many children 'consecrated' for this work who found their way to Amy's door – and before long, Amy went looking for them in the dark corners of Indian

---

1. Iain Murray, *Amy Carmichael: Beauty for Ashes* (Banner of Truth, 2015), p. 31.

society. Her rescue work with the temple children led her to full-time children's work, not only caring for the children but also fighting their legal battles and the relatives who wanted to sell their futures. She took in not only temple children but others at risk, including orphans and unwanted babies. From very early days, she was conscious of the quite practical help of angels as well as the presence of Jesus.

Amy's ministry taking care of a few little girls of various ages in her mission station expanded, over many years, into a separate multi-building complex with hundreds of girls, boys, babies, and many teachers and assistants, and even a hospital.

Her biographer Iain Murray writes:

> To all the children Amy was 'Amma' (mother). She was described, not as walking but as 'flying' to attend to the many needs. The children came to nick-name her 'the Hare'. In time she would use a tricycle to move even faster between the various buildings.[2]

Of course, Amy not only took care of the children's medical and educational needs; she sought to fill their lives with love, wonder and spiritual understanding. 'Love was the starting point, to be taught in the first instance by example. Not a child went to sleep at night without a kiss from Amy, and even when the numbers ultimately made that impossible, as long as she could, she sought to see each child every day. Commonly, the birth date of the children was unknown, so, as a substitute,

---

2.   Ibid, p. 50.

the 'Coming date' of each girl to Dohnavur was celebrated, and their bedroom decked with flowers.'[3]

Amy wrote many books about her experiences and ministry in India. She was clear-eyed about the lack of glamour in her work, and many mothers will recognise her lifestyle even without the pressures of ministry! As she wrote:

> 'Always there were hindrances, just simple and ordinary. The crush of other duties around one, the impossibility of assured quiet for even an hour at a stretch, the lack of invigorating influences – for who finds the Plains of India invigorating?' Then she added words which epitomize the story of her life, 'But I have been splendidly helped.'[4]

Amy had the correct perspective that the Lord was carrying her burdens, not she carrying His. The work she was doing for Him was only what He Himself was already employed in, and she was working under His close direction. And what fruit was borne out of that work! In 1912-13, there was a revival blowing through the compound and, in 1913 alone, thirty children were baptised. Iain Murray summarises the impact of Amy's work by the end of her life:

> Her calling as a mother meant 'cutting the toe nails of a thousand children', and doing that with a greater hope in view. For numbers that hope was to be fulfilled: 'We shall train them to live for others, not self.' Through the years, from the company of those once children, there have been those who have remained at Dohnavur to look after 'senior

---

3.   Ibid, p. 54.
4.   Ibid, p. 59.

citizens', or to nurse at the hospital which at one point annually served 1,800 in-patients, and over 60,000 out-patients, when local facilities were few. Others work with different Christian agencies, or in secular employment, and many marry and establish Christian homes.[5]

As well as being a writer, Amy was a gifted poet, and often wrote a few lines to her personal correspondents. Her motivation, and her joy, in all the intensity of her work can be found in these short lines:

> To each is given a bag of tools
> An hour glass and a book of rules,
> And each must build ere his work is done
> A stumbling block, or a stepping stone.

* * *

My son, give me your heart, and let your eyes observe my ways (Prov. 23:26).

Our overview of Amy Carmichael's life is brief, but that is for a reason. Amy does not shine so much in biography as she does in speaking for herself – and she published many books in her time on the Lord's work, especially in her beloved India. In going through her example in this chapter, we will look at her own words.

As I sat down to begin writing about Amy, I opened a little paperback collection of excerpts from her letters, called *Candles in the Darkness*. The first thing I saw when I opened the little book was the name, written in a familiar cursive script: Elizabeth Graham. Some of you reading this book

---

5.   Ibid, p. 140.

will know that name well. Elizabeth, along with her husband Bill, was a missionary in South Africa for many years, where they ran a theological college to train local pastors. Upon their return to Scotland, Elizabeth served the Free Church as faithfully and lovingly as she had tended her overseas mission field. I had the privilege to worship alongside her for nearly twenty years before her death. On each of my children's birthdays, a handwritten card would arrive in the post 'from St Columba's Free Church' – in Elizabeth's handwriting. I don't know how I came to own her copy of *Candles*, but to open it up and see her name on my first day of writing about Amy Carmichael reminded me powerfully and lovingly of the chain of nurturing throughout the Christian Church. And the chain doesn't end there, for Elizabeth's daughter Anne is one of my editors – and she now sends the birthday cards too!

Part of God's plan for the Church is that we have spiritual mentors, and we mentor others and introduce them to other women who then become part of our story. To be reminded of that in the early days of this book felt like a clear mark of God's grace. The rest of this chapter is built upon that little book, *Candles in the Darkness*, which gives us beautiful lessons drawn from Amy Carmichael's care for her adopted family and passion for her Lord.

Every Moment is Precious

Fill the crevices of time with the things that matter most. This will cost something, but it is worth it. 'Seek ye My face.

My heart said unto Thee, Thy face, Lord, will I seek.'[6] No one is of much use who does not truly want to learn what it means to pray and listen and definitely choose the life that is hid with Christ in God.

Keep close, keep close. If you are close you will be keen. Your heart will be set on the things that abide. You will drink of His spirit and you will thirst for souls even as He thirsts. You will not be attracted by the world that crucified Him, but you will love the people in that world who have never seen His beauty and are losing so much more than they know. You will live to share your joy in Him. Nothing else will count for much.

All this will be, if you walk with Him as with a visible Companion, from dawn through all the hours till you go to sleep at night. And your nights may be holy too, every waking moment a loving turning to Him who is watching over your sleep as your Mother watched over it when you were a tiny child.[7]

Whether you are working for an employer or for your own family, or simply redeeming the time during retirement or unemployment, you are working for the Lord – and you will be called on to account for the limited time you were given on this earth. In the time of the English Revival, there was a movement of evangelical students who placed emphasis on not wasting a moment of their time, but giving their all to the Lord in worship, service and study.

We work for the Lord in keeping an orderly home, in spending time in quiet reflection with Him, in serving others,

---

6.   Psalm 27:8 KJV

7.   Amy Carmichael, *Candles in the Darkness*, p. 7.

in doing everything we do well. But we also spend it in time resting well. A continual redeeming of the time does not mean endless 'doing', though it does mean a consistent and diligent 'working while it is yet day, for the night is coming, when no one can work'.[8] We must not forget that rest is a necessity for life, one which the Lord planned and instituted when He gifted man the Sabbath. So if I don't mean endless working, what does it mean to fill the crevices of time as Amy prescribes?

In my experience, there are two keys. The first is prioritisation: both of practical matters and spiritual ones. Practically, it is useful to train yourself into the pattern of someone who gets the necessary things out of the way before turning to the enjoyable things—I could not sit down and write this until I had tidied up the kitchen! Even as a child, you may have known a long delightful Saturday marred only by the knowledge that the whole weekend's homework was still waiting for you; on the other hand, it was wonderful to play knowing it was already done. But, as always, the spiritual prioritisation is even more important. I also could not sit down and write this until I had read from the Bible and committed the work to the Lord. The same should be true with the work we do serving our spiritual children. If we truly wish to draw them nearer to Christ, then we must prioritise spending time with Him ourselves, and committing both ourselves and our spiritual children to Him. His is the work, as Amy knew, and we can only participate in it meaningfully if we are submitted to Him.

---

8. John 9:4.

My second key is that of focus. We face so many distractions – competing demands, our own interests and passions, deadlines, anxieties, interruptions, notifications! Some of these only take our attention for a few moments. Others can throw us off-course for years. Some of these are necessary (by all means interrupt your prayer time for a minute if you suddenly realise you've left something in the oven too long and your smoke alarm is going off). Others are not only unnecessary but tempt us to go in the very opposite direction to

> *In every long-term distraction that we face, whether a sorrow that we can't defeat or a temptation we can't resist, the answer is always to turn our eyes back upon Christ.*

God's purposes for us. But in every long-term distraction that we face, whether a sorrow that we can't defeat or a temptation we can't resist, the answer is always to turn our eyes back upon Christ. (You'll forgive me if I can't help repeating myself that focus on Jesus is the key to every struggle in Christian life – the longer I spent writing this book, the more every chapter pointed me back to Him as the only solution!)

It helps to have particular verses or even songs which point us back to a view of who Jesus is and why He is so worthy of our love and service. One favourite of mine is Hebrews 1:3, which describes Jesus as follows:

> *He is the radiance of the glory of God and the exact imprint of his nature, and he upholds the universe by the word of his power. After making purification for sins, he sat down at the right hand of the Majesty on high.*

I have found times in my life when I've been called to set down the thing I enjoyed most – personal ambition, a writing project I loved, a hope for the immediate future – not because it was harmful, but because it was becoming my delight. I don't want anything to be my true delight except the Saviour who died for me. When I've picked those things up again, I've often found that I simply can't rest in them any longer. Hobbies and pastimes I've loved just don't feel important. And it's in those times, of giving quite benign things over to the Lord in order to carve out a larger place for Him in my life, that I have felt His presence most clearly, 'every waking moment a loving turning to Him.'

Time Spent on 'Little Things' is not a Little Thing

> Many of you are preparing for service. This is my word for you: Don't say 'It doesn't matter' about anything (except your own feelings), for everything matters. Everything is important, even the tiniest thing. If you do everything, whether great or small, for the sake of your Saviour and Lord, then you will be ready for whatever work He has chosen for you to do later.[9]

Yesterday, the baby woke up with a red, snotty face, a constant wail, and a need to be held constantly. Some days you find from the start that it isn't going to be the most productive day ever. Here's what I got done yesterday: I fed, clothed and took the older children to school. I picked up yogurt and new kid jeans at the store. I cleaned the kitchen. I wrote part of this

---

9.   Carmichael, p. 4.

chapter while the baby napped. I held him. A lot. I answered emails and did some admin. I tidied up toys, folded and put away laundry. I wiped the table and swept the floor. I played with the baby when he felt a bit better. I picked up the kids from school. I made bread, lunch and dinner and tidied up some more. I supervised bedtime, brushing teeth and wiping bottoms and breaking up arguments. At the end of the day I conducted a short interview for a magazine article and finished up doing some needlework on a quilt to relax.

I felt guilty for how little I had done.

The house looked the same as it had the night before – what you might call 'contained chaos' – and the book was not much further forward. My internal to-do list loomed over me. I have to admit, though, seeing it written down in black and white, it's kind of crazy that I felt bad about my day. My job is to make our lives run smoothly. My work is all those little things: loads of laundry and loads of dishes and a carpool service. There are many times when I have swept a floor or picked up an armful of toys fuming that I just did this a few hours ago and I will do it again a few hours later. I have fumed at the times when this work felt invisible, felt not good enough, felt mechanical and burdensome. I mean, is the floor even swept if no one notices? Why don't the family recognise the significance of not stepping on a handful of dried sweetcorn when they put their feet under the table? So much of what I do is removing messes and inconveniences that my family never knew existed in the first place (tribute to my efficiency … sometimes!). I work flat-out just to keep things ticking along normally; a special effort like cleaning out a closet or reorganising a bedroom feels herculean.

Two things have helped me find motivation in serving my family, both of them from the Lord. The first is an observation I read by another mother, and I wish I could remember who in order to credit her. The idea is that the Lord makes the sun to rise, the flowers to bloom, shapes the clouds and maintains our lot every day. Common grace is everywhere in the small details of life: the morning coffee, the song on the radio, the misfortunes that never come upon us due to His loving, unseen care. So often we treat God like kids treat the mum cleaning Lego off a floor – we don't notice our path has been cleared, but we are quick to notice and show indignation if we step on the Lego! So I have learned to see my many small daily tasks as presenting to my family 'new mercies every morning' – trying to make the world around them as pleasant and graceful as I can, just as He does for us.

> *I have learned to see my many small daily tasks as presenting to my family* 'new mercies every morning.'

The other thing the Lord has given me, after many years of defensiveness and resentment about housework, is a desire to have a clean house. I was never someone who particularly noticed a few crumbs on the floor or a streak on a window before. Finally, though, I have found that the measure of peace of mind that can be gained from a clean floor and a made bed is deeply satisfying. There are some tasks I do out of love for my family, but keeping things tidy has become like a gift God wants to give me, that I can give back to Him. I wanted the cleanliness and order of my soul, through His grace, to be reflected back to my family through the state of our home. Understand, I still have a way to go on this. I'm not a natural organiser and am totally intimidated by DIY. But the Lord has begun a good work in me and I know He brings His work to completion.

There is no Fruit without Pain

We need never, never fear that the stream of love will run dry. The heavenly river, the river of God which is full of water, never will. And so, as drop by drop we seem to be drained dry, it is only seeming. It isn't really so. It cannot be so. For more love is perpetually pouring through us, 'love instead of love'.

Your [weary] friend will find it so. All will seem to be used up, all strength, all that she has to give, and then more will come. She will reign in life – another of the words in Romans that are fathomless.

But I know well that these are hard days. His were hard. We don't want ease when He had rough ways. She is tired for His name's sake. Jesus being weary sat there on the well. How glad we shall be afterwards that we were allowed to be weary for Him.

Yes, love is a glorious thing, new every morning. There is nothing to fear if there is love. 'Lord, do Thou turn me all into love, and all my love into obedience. And let my obedience be without interruption(Saint Augustine)'.[10]

There is no kind of motherhood, physical or spiritual, which does not entail work, hard work. The work of prayer, the

---

10. Carmichael, p. 106.

healing touch, the nourishment and advice and sleeplessness, the sharing of griefs and carrying of burdens – whether they be sorrows or overloaded backpacks! And it all starts with the physical agony of labour. Don't think that this doesn't

> *There is no kind of motherhood, physical or spiritual, which does not entail work, hard work.*

apply to non-biological mothers. Labour pains are a frequent illustration used in the Bible for the very real, almost tangible hurt of pouring yourself out for the Gospel. Paul refers to the Galatians as 'my little children, for whom I am again in the anguish of childbirth until Christ is formed in you!'[11] His pain actually was physical, his body delivered up to beatings and death for the bearing of many spiritual children. Even of Jesus it is prophesied in Isaiah 53:10 that He who was made an offering for sin would 'see his offspring and prolong his days'. Pain and new life are in this way actually inextricable, even though it was Him who went through the greatest pain, so that we might have new life.

My favourite quotation from Amy Carmichael is: 'See in it a chance to die.' It is not only physical trials or persecution that allow us to participate in the sufferings and death of the Lord. It is whatever sacrifices we make for His sake. Child calling you away from a good book? *See in it a chance to die.* The person you've been mentoring shows hurtful ingratitude? *See in it a chance to die.* Someone comes to you in need and you can only give to them by denying a comfort to yourself?

---

11. Galatians 4:19.

See in it a chance to die. It is such a comfort that by giving up some of ourselves, we are following in His footsteps. And, remember, the sacrifice is worth it:

> Don't be surprised if you are set at nought [rejected; treated with contempt]. It is part of the way of the Cross. Mark 9:12 says, 'The Son of Man must be set at nought.' If we follow in the way He went, we also must be set at nought. You will find this truer every year as you go on. And anything is easier. Scourging is easier. 'He must suffer many things, and' (as if this had to be mentioned very specially) 'be set at nought.'
>
> Have you ever gone through your New Testament marking the places where the iron of suffering in one form or another is mentioned? It's wonderfully enlightening. The book is full of joy I know, but it is also full of pain, and pain is taken for granted. 'Think it not strange. Count it all joy.'
>
> We are meant to follow His steps, not avoid them. What if the suffering is caused by those whom we love? Was His not caused by those whom He loved? Oh, what a book the Bible is! If only we steep our souls in its mighty comfort we can't go far wrong – we shall never lose heart. 1 Peter 2:21: 'For hereunto were ye called; because Christ also suffered for you, leaving you an example, that ye should follow His steps.'
>
> You will find the joy of the Lord comes as you go on in the way of the Cross. It was one who had nobody all His own on earth who said, 'If I am offered upon the sacrifice and service of your faith, I joy, and rejoice' (Phil. 2:17 RV). It is no small gift of His love, this opportunity to be offered upon the sacrifice and service; something you would not naturally choose, something that asks for more than you would naturally give. That's the proof of His love. So rejoice! You

are giving Him what He asks you to give Him: the chance to show you what He can do.[12]

Part of the pain of motherhood is self-denial. I see that clearly in a story of King David and his mighty men, and the way that each sacrificed for the other:

> *David was then in the stronghold, and the garrison of the Philistines was then at Bethlehem. And David said longingly, 'Oh, that someone would give me water to drink from the well of Bethlehem that is by the gate!' Then the three mighty men broke through the camp of the Philistines and drew water out of the well of Bethlehem that was by the gate and carried and brought it to David. But he would not drink of it. He poured it out to the LORD and said, 'Far be it from me, O LORD, that I should do this. Shall I drink the blood of the men who went at the risk of their lives?' Therefore he would not drink it.*[13]

David had a craving for this particular, unreachable water. Not only for the nourishment it would give his body, but for its associations with home and the comforts of his early life in Bethlehem. He seems to drop a heavy hint to his men – 'Boy, I sure wish someone would go and get me that water' – but when it's in his hands, due to some incredible bravery on the part of his men, he realises how much more important are the lives of the people God made, and of whom He gave David charge. He shows both them and God the preciousness of their lives by pouring out the thing he desired most. A story which

---

12. Carmichael, p. 67.
13. 2 Samuel 23:14-17a.

started out as being about the courage of David's mighty men turns into a story about a loving shepherd king.

When you're raising children or intensively mentoring another Christian, the cravings can be very powerful. The craving for that hour or two of personal time in the evening, that you might go crazy without. The craving to indulge your own personal comfort that might trip someone else up (for example, you're fine having a glass of wine with dinner, but it would cause serious problems for the person you're pastoring). The craving to give easy answers instead of having a tough conversation. What is more important: your momentary comfort or someone else's safety and spiritual wellbeing?

The Lord Perfects our Imperfect Work

A few days ago, I woke up with a sort of picture in my mind. I saw myself cooking up a dinner party for Jesus. I had a feeling in this picture that everything was going wrong – the bread was bland and gluey, the meat a bit burnt, the table not quite set correctly. If you've done a lot of entertaining you know the ominous feeling of a dinner which is just not coming together to your satisfaction.

And then, I had a sense of the Lord looking lovingly at the table I had prepared, and suddenly, it looked like a beautiful feast – a Thanksgiving dinner, piled high with perfect food. I understood, as I thought about this picture throughout the day, that we offer to the Lord whatever work, whatever sacrifices we can, and sometimes they are pretty poor in our own eyes. It is His grace which perfects these small offerings and presents them as worthy gifts before His Father. We may not have given to the poor, or helped a friend, or taught a child from the Bible, or witnessed to God's work in our lives, to our own satisfaction. But He can use and multiply whatever we have done, even if it looks little in

> *But He can use and multiply whatever we have done, even if it looks little in our own eyes.*

our own eyes. Like my example above of my daily chores, it is easy to despise the day of small things. Yet so many small, forgettable details build up into a big picture in our spiritual child's mind of what it looks like to love and follow Jesus Christ.

> You know Campbell Morgan's thought about ministry being different from words. He sees it as the unofficial, untabulated little loving kindnesses of life. I looked the word up in Young's Concordance. It's the word used of Martha preparing food for our Lord Jesus, such an ordinary, everyday sort of thing, nothing she would expect to be remembered.
>
> He remembers every single little inconspicuous thing – quite apart from the big things, the 'works'. What a loving memory He has.[14]

My picture of The Feast has helped me to understand God's wondrous acceptance of the small tokens of love I offer Him. But we must always remember that what matters to Him is our heart. Just as 'if I give away all I have ... but have not love, I gain nothing,'[15] we really do spoil our feast if we offer our

---

14. Carmichael, p. 33.
15. 1 Corinthians 13:3.

gifts reluctantly and sourly. There are many dinner parties which are saved by the happy company around the table – and many ruined by an exhausted and resentful hostess. So whatever tasks I can fit into my day, whatever writing I can get done, whatever I can teach my children as we walk along the way, I am learning to do them willingly and contentedly as my offering to the Lord. This is my work – this is His work. It will be enough. He could make the bread and fishes into enough for five thousand and He can use my little, and your little.

This principle of Jesus perfecting our work translates also into the highest sphere in which we serve Him, that of saving souls. There can be few more painful things for a spiritual mother than to see her children wander away, or even deliberately turn away, from the Lord. As spiritual mothers, we may well feel that our work has not been enough, that we are responsible for those souls. Yet, as Amy Carmichael knew, it is only Jesus who has the power to call people to Himself, and our work is to present Him to our children:

> A few evenings ago I was reading about our Lord Jesus in the high priest's house, where He was so cruelly handled that one can hardly bear to think of more pain for Him. And then came poor Peter's denial, and He heard that denial. It must have been a thousand times more hurting than any other thing that night. 'And the Lord turned and looked on Peter.' Soon afterwards those loving eyes were blindfolded.
>
> I thought, 'If in a few minutes my eyes were to be blindfolded, how should I wish to use them before that was done?' And I remembered some of you who are wandering further from Him than Peter wandered. Oh to be able to

turn and look on them! But I cannot. They are not in the room with me. And then I remembered, He can; He does. Even now, as my heart longs over them, His heart is longing with a far greater longing. And in His eyes is something that can never be in mine: power to convict, to recall. Think of those eyes that were blindfolded. Put your name where I leave a blank space: 'And the Lord turned and looked upon _____.' May the next words be true of you: 'And _____ went out and wept bitterly.'[16]

So many times I have felt that devastating gaze of Christ upon me. And if He can awaken me with that look, then so He can awaken those whom we love. Remember that He uses us to do His work, but He doesn't need us to do His work. He so often uses ways that we could not even anticipate to accomplish His purposes, as if He delights in surprising us! We mothers are those who sow, or who water, but it is always He who gives the increase. Even if our work has been imperfect, our imperfections simply do not have the ability to destroy His purposes. And He loves and knows all our spiritual children so much better than we do. As Amy marvels, 'If [they are] so dear to me, what to Him?'[17]

Even if our work has been imperfect, our imperfections simply do not have the ability to destroy His purposes.

---

16. Carmichael, p. 21.
17. Ibid, p. 115.

Jesus is our Guide

The most important form of guidance Jesus gave His followers was by example, in deed and in prayer and in attitude. He prayed in front of them and gave them a model by which to pray. He washed their feet and told them to do the same. He condemned the proud but extended opportunity for repentance to the poor and the disgraced. He laid down His life, showing us that there is no price too high to pay for showing love to others. When they had observed Him for a while, He guided them to do what He does:

> *And he called the twelve together and gave them power and authority over all demons and to cure diseases, and he sent them out to proclaim the kingdom of God and to heal. And he said to them, 'Take nothing for your journey, no staff, nor bag, nor bread, nor money; and do not have two tunics. And whatever house you enter, stay there, and from there depart. And wherever they do not receive you, when you leave that town shake off the dust from your feet as a testimony against them.' And they departed and went through the villages, preaching the gospel and healing everywhere.[18]*

Jesus encouraged His disciples to live by faith, expecting their needs to be met moment by moment. They were not to take an anxious thought for themselves or over-prepare for their ministry, but to trust confidently that He would supply their needs, from the clothes on their backs to their food to the very words they would speak. In the same way, He lived with no worldly possessions, no home, no earthly security.

---

18. Luke 9:1-6.

Jesus guided his disciples to uncomfortable and, above all, unexpected places; He did not always explain why, but expected obedience nevertheless. The Holy Spirit had done the same for Him, leading Him into the wilderness

There is no good trying to guess ahead of time how the Lord will accomplish His purposes. Often, they will be harder than we ever imagined, and often more gracious and comforting than we had any hope they would be.

to be hungry and tempted immediately after His baptism. There is no good trying to guess ahead of time how the Lord will accomplish His purposes. Often, they will be harder than we ever imagined, and often more gracious and comforting than we had any hope they would be. We must always be looking out for His leading; we can quench the Holy Spirit despite the very best of intentions if we are determined to do God's work in our own precious way.

Verses on Guidance

He leads me in paths of righteousness for his name's sake ... your rod and your staff, they comfort me (Ps. 23:3, 4b).

You perhaps do not fully appreciate the comfort of the 'rod and staff' until you have felt utterly perplexed by life. If you think you can rely on your own wisdom, you may meet the Lord's guidelines and restraints with a sense of irrelevance or resentment. When you realise that you have no idea how you got your life into such a mess or what you do from here, you long for God's wisdom and help. And He always answers, 'without rebuke,'[19] to show you how to live in His ways:

> *And your ears shall hear a word behind you, saying, 'This is the way, walk in it,' when you turn to the right or when you turn to the left* (Isa. 30:21).

How do you hear God's voice when you are making a decision? The answer is not usually an audible word. His voice comes to us most clearly in the Scripture. But He does speak in other ways – through our conscience, through opened doors, through a sense of leading, through unusual circumstances (though every subjective experience of 'His voice' must be measured against Scripture, which is our only totally dependable way of hearing Him). The comfort I do take from this, though, is that as long as we are seeking Him whole-heartedly, He will not let us step outside of His plan.

> *I will ask the Father, and he will send you another Helper, to be with you forever ... I will not leave you as orphans; I will come to you* (John 14:16-18).

The Holy Spirit does so much. He comforts, helps, guides, prays, convicts, encourages, strengthens, empowers, prompts, and dwells with us and in us and alongside us. He is the goodness of God living in our very souls, transforming them daily. If Jesus is Immanuel, God *with* us, the Holy Spirit is God *in* us.

---

19. James 1:5.

Questions

1. What distractions, anxieties or temptations do you need to subdue so that you can more fully focus upon Jesus and His work for you?

2. What are some of the small, dull or relentless tasks you find difficult to do with a willing and cheerful spirit? How can you find a way to do those things unto the Lord, and in such a way as to point others to Him?

3. Are there sacrifices you are called to make as you serve others for the Lord? If so, give thanks for these and use them to reflect upon His sacrifice for you. Are there other things in which He is calling you to 'see a chance to die'?

Be thou my vision, O Lord of my heart
Naught be all else to me, save that thou art;
Thou my best thought, by day or by night;
Waking or sleeping, thy presence my light.
– Mary Byrne

3. A Persistent Mother

Monica

Monica, who gave birth physically and spiritually to Augustine of Hippo, is one of the best-known mothers in Christian history. Although a Roman Catholic, her example as spiritual mother and evangelist to her son – in both theology and example – are replete with lessons for any woman who knows Christ. In *Feminine Threads: Women in the Tapestry of Christian History*, Diana Severance provides a succinct summary of Monica's life and influence:

> Monica was cared for by an old maidservant who had cared for her father when he was a child. This servant was noted for her Christian and moral character and care for all the daughters in the family. She was more important than their mother in the instruction and training she provided.
>
> Monica's husband Patricius could be both kind and quick-tempered, and, acceptable to the mores of the day, often unfaithful to Monica. ... As Augustine later wrote, Monica spoke of Christ to Patricius 'through her virtues' by which Christ had made her beautiful. She never quarrelled

with Patricius about his infidelities, hoping that once he converted to Christianity he would become chaste. She never opposed him when he was angry but waited until he calmed down to explain her actions, if they had caused the offense. Patricius could not help but respect and love her.

Monica was a servant of servants, caring for all as if they were her children. She cared for her parents and her family with Christian devotion. She brought up three children – Augustine, his brother Navigius, and a sister traditionally named Perpetua – and endured travail as they all went astray. Yet, before her death, all were bound together in the community of Christ. Patricius converted to Christianity before his death, was baptized and led a life befitting a Christian thereafter. When Patricius died Augustine was sixteen, and starting to become wayward. Patricius' salvation encouraged Monica just at the time Augustine's rebelliousness began.

Patricius was little concerned about the morality of his children, so it was Monica who warned the youthful Augustine about the sins of fornication and adultery. Augustine scorned her advice.

Augustine began seeking meaning and purpose in life more in secular education than in Christian teaching. For a time he became a Manichean ... similar to Gnosticism in its emphasis on intellectual knowledge. Monica recognised that Augustine was spiritually 'in the grip of death' by his adherence to this false faith. She refused to let her son live in the house any more, so repulsed was she by the error of the Manicheans. About that time, however, she had a dream encouraging her to allow Augustine to eat at her table. The vision was of her weeping for Augustine's perdition, and a young man appearing asked her the cause of her weeping. The young man told her to observe that where she was,

Augustine was also. When Monica told Augustine about the vision, he tried to twist the vision to say she would join him in the Manichean belief. She responded, 'No, the vision was, you will be where I am!' Monica's quick reply affected Augustine more than the dream itself had. Monica took comfort in this dream that predicted the joy of Augustine's ultimate salvation, though he continued to wander in unbelief for nine more years.

When Augustine did come to faith in Christ, he was baptised by Ambrose in the church where Monica had often prayed for his soul. Her grief turned to joy. With her son's salvation, she felt she was no longer needed on earth. When Augustine, Monica, and their group decided to return to Africa, they stopped at the Italian port of Ostia. Augustine and Monica conversed together about eternity, recalling that 'eye has not seen, nor ear heard, neither have entered into the heart of man, the things which God hath prepared for them that love Him' (1 Cor. 2:9, KJV). They shared a vision of the Eternal, climbing step by step beyond the corporeal senses so that the world and its delights became worthless. Monica shortly after became ill of a fever and died before sailing. She was 56, and Augustine was 33.

... Though as a mother she was marred by a lack of firm discipline and by having worldly ambitions for her son, she continues to be an example of a mother whose heart for God and unceasing prayers for her children were constant. She lived to see her son become a Christian. She could not know the deep influence her son would have on Christians in his own day and for centuries to come.[1]

---

1.   This section is from *Feminine Threads*, Christian Focus. I cannot recommend this book highly enough for anyone interested in the history of women throughout the Church.

* * *

And this is the confidence that we have toward him, that if we ask anything according to his will he hears us (1 John 5:14).

A Praying Mother

There are few things more daunting to talk about in a book about living the Christian life than your prayer habits. I don't think I have ever met anyone who felt that they prayed enough, or that they prayed well. Prayer is the greatest power we have, and yet we find it mysterious and difficult and even dull (all of which suggest we have a lot to learn!). Perhaps we may go through a time of more intense prayer when times are hard. But when life is going well, instead of making up that painful fervour in adoration and thanksgiving, we turn to other interests and distractions.

No doubt the reason we struggle so much to maintain a consistent prayer life is that we think of prayer as something we do, instead of turning to prayer as a natural reaction to who God is. Good prayer often begins in the Bible, as we are pointed back to Him.

> *No doubt the reason we struggle so much to maintain a consistent prayer life is that we think of prayer as something we do, instead of turning to prayer as a natural reaction to who God is.*

We struggle to pray well for our spiritual children for many reasons. They themselves are often demanding and distracting. In times of exhaustion we can turn to 'survival mode' rather than pouring time into intercession. We find it easy to lose sight of the souls in our care as eternal beings, with eternal

We find it easy to lose sight of the souls in our care as eternal beings, with eternal destinations, and purposes set by God before birth.

destinations, and purposes set by God before birth. Monica was a godly woman who knew the importance of these things and was passionate in bringing her children before the Lord.

After his conversion, Augustine said:

'My mother placed great hope in [God],' and she 'was in greater labour to ensure my salvation than she had been at my birth.' Amidst years of tearful prayers, Monica became convinced that her wayward son would eventually return to the Church. She believed God had promised as much in a personal vision and had confirmed this promise through the prophetic words of her bishop, who proclaimed, 'It cannot be that the son of these tears should be lost.'

He seemed to marvel over the depth of his mother's prayer life for him:

You put forth your hand from on high, and you drew my soul out of that pit of darkness, when before you my mother, your faithful servant, wept more for me than mothers weep over their children's dead bodies. By that spirit of faith which she had from you, she saw my death, and you graciously heard her, O Lord. Graciously you hear her, and you did not despise her tears when they flowed down from her eyes and watered the earth beneath, in whatsoever place she prayed.[2]

---

2. These quotations from https://aleteia.org/2021/08/27/discover-monica-in-augustines-confessions/. The whole of Augustine's Confessions

When Monica finally received the answer she prayed for so long, and Augustine surrendered to the Lord, she did not then ease off on her prayer life. Instead, she and her son built one another up in a glorious shared passion for their Saviour's grace and goodness, magnifying and enjoying Him. The overflow of all those years of pleading was uncontained in the mother's joy over her spiritual child.[3]

I wrote a poem a few years ago about the exhaustion of prayer life when surrounded by small children. Whenever I come across it, it reminds me of the importance of praying even when one is too tired to think. Whatever stage your spiritual child is at, whatever their level of maturity and need, these days are short and will not come again. Prayer and discipleship are for now.

> *These days are short and will not come again. Prayer and discipleship are for now.*

---

can be accessed for free at https://www.gutenberg.org/files/3296/3296-h/3296-h.htm

3. A sweet memorial remains to the spiritual connection finally enjoyed by Monica and her son: *On the Happy Life,* a classical dialogue Augustine recorded (basically a philosophical conversation) between himself, some friends, and his mother. After a long discussion, it is Monica who finally drives home the great point, that there is no happiness without wisdom, and wisdom is inseparable from Christ. 'Here,' Augustine writes, 'when all cried out with wonder, I myself was also not a little bit delighted and glad that she had said the most powerful thing, which, as a great thing from the books of the philosophers, I had planned to bring out last.' Monica was finally vindicated by her son on a mental, emotional and spiritual level, while enjoying the far greater satisfaction of knowing him to be saved by Christ. *On the Happy Life: St Augustine's Cassiciacum Dialogues, volume 2.* Michael P. Foley, ed. (Yale University Press: New Haven & London), 2019.

When my children are grown
I'll have time to pray for them.
When they can shut up long enough for me to string two
blessed thoughts together
I will pray to be a more patient mother.
When they can listen to a whole Bible story
and ask intelligent questions
Then I'll read them the Bible
(And when I can get through a whole Psalm
without falling asleep
I'll read it too).
I'll play with them when they stop cheating at Candy Land.
I'll listen when they can talk calmly instead of whining.
I'll kiss them when they've learned not to slobber on my
cheek.
Yet prayer won't wait because they won't wait
Even if I can't string two prayers together –
Just same time, same place, every morning in the car
Every night, sticky fingers splayed over sleepy eyes.
Help her be kind
Keep him safe by the road
Thank you, oh thank you that they are sleeping.
Waiting to pray is like waiting for the day
They no longer want kisses, and pull away
Before you pull them back for one more kiss
On that curly head.

A Patient Mother

We have discussed at length the hard work, prayer and
sacrifice needed to spiritually nurture another person. But we
have not touched on one of the elements that keeps us going.

Of the three virtues named by Paul – faith, hope and love – it perhaps receives the least focus in our lives. *Hope.*

Hope is a gift from God. It is also a spiritual discipline such as it took Monica many years to hone. When things are looking down, we naturally tend to gloom and pessimism. And our expectations so often affect our actions. If we believe we are incapable of finishing a project, we probably won't persist with it. If we believe we can't win the race, we won't put our whole effort into running. And if we lose hope that God can work in the people around us, we will slowly stop praying, stop seeking to offer them a better future, stop calling them to account, stop sympathizing, stop offering help, stop pointing them to Christ. Without hope, our hearts grow cold. *They'll never change. They're a lost cause. They'll always be miserable. They'll never believe.* That voice is not the voice of God, but of the Accuser!

Hope is a gift from God. It is also a spiritual discipline.

Without hope, our hearts grow cold.

When we have been disappointed by a child or friend, when we see them making poor decisions or failing to repent of sin or refusing help, it's discouraging. We can lose hope in our child. But then, our faith is not in our child. Our faith is in the Lord! People rarely change themselves; and when they do, they change their behaviour, not their hearts. It is the Lord who changes us. It is Him who opens people's eyes (who opened our eyes) to see themselves, who calls them by name, who offers them hope. So often, the people who challenge our ability to hope are those who have themselves lost hope in their own future – or who have built their future so much in the things of this world that they see no need of hope for any spiritual things at all.

Monica, upset and overwhelmed by her son actually casting his lot with a worldly philosophy instead of with the Lord she loved, was tempted to write him off completely. The pain of seeing him lost was too much to bear; and she was indignant, both on the Lord's behalf and no doubt feeling rejected herself in the way she had taught him. She believed in that moment that she had reached the end of the story.

It took the Lord's intervention to restore hope to Monica. We see the gift and the discipline of hope working together: He gave her a particular word, through a dream, that she would yet see Augustine in fellowship with Jesus and restored to herself as well. But once she had received that dream, she had the spiritual self-discipline to keep hold of hope.

> A ... noteworthy aspect of Monica's piety was her confidence in the Lord. Once she received a dream confirming that her son would one day become a Christian, she appeared to rest in this promise. Her unwavering confidence was evident in the noticeable change in her demeanor and strategy toward Augustine after the dream. When she learned of her son's rejection of the Manichees, for example, she calmly viewed it as only the beginning of his transformation. While Monica had taken matters into her own hands in Thagaste and frequently implored her bishop to speak with her son, in Milan she seemed to wait quietly on the Lord, even with

the eloquent Ambrose available as a resource. Her faith had matured and it altered her approach to her wayward son.[4]

Not only did Monica practise hope in what she believed God had said to her, but she also sought reassurance and confirmation from her own spiritual mentors. None of the personal assurances or messages we may feel we receive from God bear the weight of Scripture. They must always be tested, be accepted with an understanding that the Word, not our own experience, is supreme. Sometimes we will 'hear wrong'. Sometimes, the Lord will accomplish the answer to our prayer in a completely different way to what we expect. As we grow in discernment, we can make use of those who spiritually pastor us and who will drive us to keep on hoping.

Sometimes, the Lord will accomplish the answer to our prayer in a completely different way to what we expect.

God did not see it as the end of the story when Adam and Eve listened to the serpent instead of to His will for them. They made a bad decision, one that we re-enact every day of our lives. But rather than leaving His world to condemnation and eternal death, the Lord immediately sparked hope. There would be death, but not forever. There would be

But rather than leaving His world to condemnation and eternal death, the Lord immediately sparked hope.

4. https://equip.sbts.edu/publications/journals/journal-of-discipleship-and-family-ministry/jdfm-41-spring/so-many-voices-the-piety-of-monica-mother-of-augustine/

condemnation of sin, but not of His people. A rescuer would come. There was a time in each of our lives when we were at the end of our story – living for ourselves and our idols – and we needed that Rescuer. For each of us, even those who came to faith at a young age, the Lord has been so patient. He has been patient for us to come to Him, patient for us to grow in Him, patient as He waits for us to repent, patient as He calls us to participate in His word, patient as He waits for us to surrender again and again. He can be patient because of the hope He gives, the hope He is. Hope is the endgame of patience; they are inseparable. And the animus that links these two great gifts is waiting with persistence.

A Persistent Mother

Why are we so surprised at the prominence of waiting in our prayer lives? The Bible prepares us for it. The stories of Bible heroes are in a fairly condensed form, so in the course of a few verses we seem to skip over the twenty-five years Abraham waited for the son of promise, or the years Joseph waited in slavery and prison before being elevated over his brothers, or the three weeks of fasting before the angel Gabriel appeared to Daniel, or the seventy years of repentance during the Babylonian captivity, or the four hundred years between the last Old Testament prophets and the Lord's word coming to Zechariah the father of John the Baptist.

God accomplishes His purposes, but He doesn't rush them. He needs us to see, when we have run out of our own strategies and our own strength and patience, that we must be completely reliant on Him. The waiting is part of the answer: that is where so much of our growing happens.

> *The waiting is part of the answer: that is where so much of our growing happens.*

And yet there are other times when we experience the greatness of His grace. As the Lord says in Isaiah 65:24:

> *'Even before they call, I will answer, and while they are still speaking I will hear'* (BSB).

If we can call it to mind, most of us have undoubtedly had this experience too. God always knows what we need before we even ask for it. He does not always make us wait; I have had times He has provided for a need before I even knew it would arise. His timing, whether it is pre-emptive or means a long wait, is always part of His goodness to us.[5]

In John chapter 11, Jesus hears that His dear friend Lazarus is very ill. When He hears that Lazarus is dying, although He loves him and his sisters Mary and Martha dearly, Jesus waits two more days before going to them. Except that the passage, as I've quoted it, is not quite right. He didn't linger 'although' He loved them. Here is John 11:5-6:

> *Now Jesus loved Martha and her sister and Lazarus. So, when he heard that Lazarus was ill, he stayed two days longer in the place where he was.*

Did you ever notice that 'so' – that 'because'? I never did, until a friend in a Bible study pointed it out. You can rearrange the

---

5. This section first published in *The Record*, Free Church of Scotland, December 2021: 'Heart Apologetics: Why Doesn't God Answer Prayer?', article mine.

clauses: 'Because He loved Martha and her sister and Lazarus … He stayed two days longer.' To quote my friend, Carlee, directly:

'Jesus did not want to show these people, whom He loved, one of His usual healings. For them He had a sign of something far greater: His power over death itself, which He would soon manifest in His own body.'

I have seen such waiting periods in my own life, and Monica did in hers, and perhaps you have as well. Those situations where prayers are met with long-delayed answers, only for God to show His power and grace much more gloriously than if He had granted our requests right away. And often, as we wait for the outcome of our prayer, we are given other 'answers' along the way. We may not have prayed for patience or tenderness or discernment directly, but these may be some of the things God wants to grow in us as we wait on Him. Don't waste the waiting!

Where do we see Jesus Showing Persistence?

Jesus leaves the ninety-nine safe sheep of His flock to go and seek the one who has lost its way.[6] A bruised reed He will not break, and a faintly burning wick He will not quench.[7]

The wandering, the rebellious, the foolish, and the worldly all find redemption through Him who seeks their souls.[8]

---

6.   Luke 15, cf. Matthew 18.

7.   Isaiah 42:3 – and how easy it is to be that faltering reed or wick which once was strong and bright!

8.   Psalm 107, 'The Psalm of the redeemed'.

When the Lord Jesus called a self-righteous young man called Saul on the Damascus road, He said, 'It is hard for you to kick against the goads' (like an ox trying to escape from its yoke).[9] He knew Saul's heart and conscience, and stepped in with a discerning and devastating word just at the right time. The Lord allowed Saul to persist in wickedness for a time, but intervened when it would give Him the most glory. What could be more impossible than a notorious persecutor of the Church fully repenting and spreading the Good News about Jesus throughout the Roman empire? Yet nothing is impossible with God!

After three years with His disciples, answering their questions, rebuking their misperceptions, making peace between arguing factions, and reshaping their ambitions, the book of John says, 'having loved his own who were in the world, he loved them unto the end'.[10] What was the end? Washing the feet of those who were born in enmity to Him, and laying down His life to make them His. How many ways have we ourselves been objects of the Lord's loving persistence? And if we do not know Him yet, behold, He stands at the door and knocks. If anyone hears His voice, and opens the door, He will come in and eat with her, and her with Him.[11]

Verses on the Lord who is Hope

God does not want us to live with a sense of doom, despair or dread.[12] He gives us hope for eternal life,[13] hope for release from

---

9.   Acts 26:14.
10.   John 13:1.
11.   Revelation 3:20.
12.   2 Timothy 1:7.
13.   Titus 1:2.

sin and curse,[14] hope that we will reign with Him,[15] hope that He will perfect what He has begun in us,[16] hope that He will find us a 'good and faithful servant' worthy of reward,[17] and hope that our trials and discipline will not be for nothing but will produce for us a 'good future' which serves the Lord's plan.[18]

My favourite verses on 'hope' speak of the hope of forgiveness, fellowship with God, and deliverance. Psalm 130:

Out of the depths I cry to you, OLord!
O Lord, hear my voice!
Let your ears be attentive
to the voice of my pleas for mercy!
If you, O Lord, should mark iniquities,
O Lord, who could stand?
But with you there is forgiveness,
that you may be feared.
I wait for the Lord, my soul waits,
and in his word I hope;
my soul waits for the Lord
more than watchmen for the morning,
more than watchmen for the morning.

---

14. Romans 8:18-25, with special emphasis on v. 24, '*For in this hope we were saved. Now hope that is seen is not hope. For who hopes for what he sees?*' This is a beautiful intersection of hope with faith.

15. 2 Timothy 2:12.

16. Psalm 138:8.

17. Matthew 25:21.

18. Jeremiah 29:11 is a very famous verse: '*I have plans to prosper and not to harm you, to give you hope and a future*' (NIV). Note that, in context, it is reassuring a people who are facing a time of severe discipline. The Lord has not forgotten them! So the intent here is not to give assurance of worldly prosperity but of a continuing place in the Lord's purposes despite being in a hard situation. How hopeful is that!

O Israel, hope in the Lord!
For with the Lord there is steadfast love,
and with him is plentiful redemption.
And he will redeem Israel from all his iniquities.

Questions

1. Where do you struggle to maintain hope for the spiritual children (or other loved ones) in your life? Like Peter, do you find it easy to take your eyes off Jesus and onto the wind and waves even after experiencing the Lord's power?

2. Rewrite 'When my children are grown' in relation to your own spiritual children. What weariness, tenderness and burdens do you carry for them?

3. Are there 'character fruits' that God has produced in you or in those around you through a time of waiting? Can you think of an instance when having to wait for an answer has served to glorify God more than acting on our own timescale?

Softly and tenderly Jesus is calling
Calling for you and for me
See on the portals He's waiting and watching
Watching for you and for me.

Come home, come home
Ye who are weary come home
Earnestly, tenderly Jesus is calling
Calling, 'O sinner, come home.'
– Will L. Thompson

4. A Mother who Mentors

Sharon Dickens

Sharon Dickens is the Director of Women's Ministry for 20schemes, a church-planting and revitalisation ministry in Scotland. I'm going to make a confession to start out this chapter: I am Sharon's first-port-of-call editor when she writes a book. I'm not, however, sharing her story and ministry because of some publishing mutual-appreciation 'club' or corporate kickback (the book I'll be speaking about isn't produced by my publisher), but because going through her books leaves me uncomfortably challenged and also longing to minister to women, and be ministered to, the way she does. In *Unconventional: A Practical Guide to Women's Ministry in the Local Church*[1], Sharon has written a clear, systematic, honest guide to mentorship, accountability and service toward other women. We'll look at Sharon's teaching, but first she will tell

---

1. Sharon Dickens, *Unconventional: A Practical Guide to Women's Ministry in the Local Church* (10Publishing, forthcoming). Unless otherwise noted, all quotes in this chapter are from Sharon's forthcoming book.

us about how Christ has worked in her life and how she came to women's ministry:

> The one thing that the Lord has taught me the most is that nothing is wasted. When you look back in hindsight you see the purpose in everything; when you're younger you can't see it. Even when I've hated my circumstances, God has been using them to teach me.
>
> Through chronic illness, the breakdown of my marriage, and bringing kids up single-handedly, everything has taught me to be more sin-aware of myself and recognise my need to rely on God. It has also given me more empathy pastorally.
>
> So, how did a girl from a housing scheme, who knew nothing about Jesus, come to faith? As a young woman, I was dating this guy who was part of a very complex family. He had never known his father well, but wanted to start a relationship with his dad, and we went to meet him and his new wife. His father had just become a born-again Christian, and I thought this was weird. He would say bizarre things like, 'God brought me a washing machine!' It didn't make much sense to me, but we carried on meeting them regularly. We'd babysit their six kids while they went to Bible study, and then they'd come back and tell us what they'd learnt.
>
> My relationship with my boyfriend was very unhealthy, but then he got saved and that really melted my head. He was instantly transformed and I just couldn't understand that. The man I knew no longer existed. I struggled with the change in my boyfriend and the truth about Jesus – it's hard to deny Jesus is real when you see a transformed life before your eyes.
>
> I don't remember the day I was saved, but I remember the precise moment. I was wrestling with God and suddenly

understood it was really true that God actually loved me and had given His Son for me. I had no problem recognising that I was a sinner but what blew my mind was God's love – it transformed me too.

That's when life got complicated. None of my family was saved, and I was a stupid young Christian who went in wielding the gospel like a truncheon! Truth be told, they thought I was in a cult. In the six months after I got saved, a lot changed. My boyfriend and I got engaged, then split up when I sensed God saying that our marriage was not His plan. And then there was the job situation.

I'm from a scheme, so the idea is 'up and out' – I had been good at school, and my family had tried so hard to help me. I'd just qualified as an architectural technician, and suddenly I gave up my job and went to work as an intern for Edinburgh City Mission. I lived by faith, working as a support worker with their ministry to homeless people, and my family thought I was insane. I was giving up what they thought was the answer.

Over the next few years I faced completely different challenges. I married a Christian man, and we moved to different cities doing front-line homeless work, but sadly the marriage developed serious problems and didn't survive. The kids and I moved back to Edinburgh, where I had family. We struggled financially, yet God was always faithful. I told Him, 'I can't do this on my own' – and then I read about widows and orphans in the Old Testament, and how God provides for them. I felt that level of isolation and hardship, and I knew God would have to minister to us in the same way. My kids had a really hard time when we moved back up to Edinburgh. Whether it was dealing with the divorce or going to work, every decision I made was about them.

Thankfully, God gave me the most flexible job on the planet! I was now training people who were doing what I had done – teaching and creating resources to prevent homelessness. I did that for four years.

I felt broken when I moved back to Edinburgh. We couldn't find a church that really fit us, and I was determined not to go back to Niddrie, where I had served and worshipped previously, even though I felt drawn there. I wanted to sit in a pew and not be noticed, instead of being back in a church community where I was known! For weeks, I knew that God wanted me to go back – and I made excuses. 'They've moved building and I don't even know where they're meeting anymore!', I remember saying to God. 'If you want me to go, you'll have to give me an introduction.' An introduction? Almost immediately, I found myself sitting on the bus next to a lady who attended Niddrie, and who promptly invited me along.

Once I submitted to God's leading, I found the church family and love we were looking for. A couple of the men took my son under their wing, babysitting, taking him to football and helping with homework. Christians there saw our need and filled it. They gave me a place to serve, too; we had a youth group where they would let me bring my kids, even when they were too young to attend themselves. As a single mum who wanted to be actively serving at church, there were not a lot of other opportunities – but, it turns out, in the waiting God teaches you something about yourself. And everything changed one autumn when our new minister arrived, with a totally different vision for the church.[2]

---

2.   From an interview on 10/02/22.

Sharon's story continues in her new book ...

Mez McConnell arrived in September and started talking to me about working at Niddrie Community Church in October. Honestly, I was surprised at first – I always suspected he'd been pre-warned about certain 'problem women' in our church and I'm fairly certain I was at the top of that list ... Mez received some serious flack for employing me (not only from within our fellowship but other Christians leaders also). I was a female, divorced and the single parent of two kids. 'Think of the example!'

... everyone seems to have this crazy ideal, the image of what the perfect women's worker looks like – when actually the perfect women's worker for your church might be some proper random (like me), sitting in the pew waiting to be offered the chance to fly. I know that a feisty, strong-minded, gobby single parent who was divorced and carrying a trunk-load of baggage doesn't seem like the ideal candidate for a women's worker. I agreed. Even I would have suggested someone else. Truthfully, it has taken me over a decade to realise that the DNA of our women's ministry at Niddrie and 20schemes would have looked completely different with someone else driving it forward ... I don't think I'm the 'perfect' women's worker, but I am who God chose for the job.

* * *

Is Mentoring for me?

This chapter may be especially helpful for those of you who are not biological or adoptive mothers and are wondering how this whole book applies to you! I want to note, however, that it is not just for those women. Whether you have children or not, and no matter how stretched you feel in your current circumstances, whether it's toddlers or loneliness keeping you awake at night, you are still called to minister to the whole body of Christ. There are many ways of doing that, depending on the season you are in and the gifts you've been given, but becoming a real and present and personal part of someone's life is one of the most powerful ways you can serve the Lord. He does not mature us in the faith just for our own benefit, but so that we can bless and teach others.

Welcome to my Life

As a mother with small kids pretty much always in tow, I don't have a lot of opportunity to meet up for private conversations with new Christians. The same may be true of you if you're a teacher struggling to mark papers after a full day's work, or a doctor working all hours, or any number of other circumstances. When you can't carve time out of your life to meet someone in a coffee shop for an hour and a half once a week, what can you do? Give up on the Lord's plan for discipleship? No – *invite women into your life.*

How do you do that? Just do what you're doing, and invite someone to do it with you. 'Come with me to Costco; we'll get a chance to chat and share some pizza.' 'I'm taking the kids to the park – come along and walk with me.' 'I've got to be on your side of town for an appointment; can I drop in for a coffee?'

My personal favourite relationship-builder is asking for help. Many times, I've asked female students at church to come over while my husband was out, to help put the kids to bed and then hang out. One young woman got roped into helping me wrap our Christmas presents one year, and before we knew it, my home was her home-away-from-home. You're older and need groceries on a stormy day? Ask a local woman from the church to run to the shops for you, and then invite her in for a cup of tea.

My personal favourite relationship-builder is asking for help.

In my city context, it's easy getting to know young people. You're living in halls but you miss having your own kitchen? Come and bake something; you can use my flour and eggs. You're far away and homesick? I want to hear all about it. In a countryside or village context, you might have different opportunities. Someone's water is off and they need a place to shower – great, invite them in. An elderly woman needs a ride to the hospital – that's an opportunity. Once another Christian is in your life, whether you're doing a formal mentorship or not, you are building a relationship, building trust, and you'll get increasing chances to have a real conversation that opens up hearts and opens up heaven.

Sharon says this about bringing newer Christians into your everyday life:

> As godly, mature women we need to show other women how to deal well with the trials we face. To do that we need to invite them into our lives and homes. Even when our homes are messy and our kids are running riot. They need to see what it looks like for a godly, mature woman to cope well when life is chucking bricks, the kids are kicking off, and you're having a bad hair day. One who examples steadfastness, spiritual

joy, and trust ultimately examples Christ in those moments. This is where it gets uncomfortable, because all too often we find the façade and our private space comfortable. It protects us and our image. We like the idea of discipleship when it's clean, structured and doesn't really require too much personal sacrifice. We don't like it when it's messy, demanding and encroaches into our lives.

At times, Sharon reminds us in the book, we will mess up. People we are trying to lead will see us behaving in an unChristlike way, will see our mistakes and bad decisions, will see our impatience or spiritual struggle. That's okay. Their faith does not depend on our perfection, but on Christ's. But sometimes their Christian practice does depend on our example, especially if they don't know many other Christians. So they need to see repentance. They need to see responsibility and apology and grace at work. And when they mess up, when they hurt us, when they lie, when they make rookie mistakes, they need to see forgiveness. If they never get close enough to see us repent or forgive, they are missing out on some of the most important things we can teach them.

Having the Hard Conversations

There is no sinking feeling quite as exquisite as the one you get when the Lord is prodding you to start a conversation you really don't want to have. Some folks think of Christians as judgmental, but I don't think I know a single one who enjoys confronting another believer about some sin in their life. We are at a place in society where we are especially fearful of giving offence. In these times it is important to remember we are not telling people how we think they are to live, or that we are going to punish them in some way if they make decisions we find distasteful. Rather, we are pointing them to the way God says will be fulfilling, peaceful and honouring to Him. If these are things that aren't important to your spiritual child, then there are heart issues deeper than whatever particular attitude or outward sin they are manifesting. Sharon has some hard words for those of us who are tempted to avoid conflict at any cost.

> **Teach biblical truth:** Do we challenge the addiction, the sexual immorality, the idol of comfort, theft, the misuse of money, their purity or gossip? Honestly, it can feel daunting. We may feel out of our depth, but we need to trust God and His word.
>
> ... When we teach the whole counsel of God, it is his word and the Holy Spirit that convicts those we are discipling. He picks the agenda and where you start. Trust Him. God in His infinite wisdom knows exactly where to prod and challenge. He knows exactly what area of life He wants to address and tackle first. We simply need to consistently teach the word of God and who Jesus is.
>
> **We need to get to the HEART of the matter.** Christians suck at this – we dance around an issue, never quite getting to the point or being clear because we don't want to cause offence, embarrassment or upset anyone. We need to love well enough to ask the hard, painful, challenging questions and not avoid them because it makes us uncomfortable.
> For some, even when there is serious sin, all too often we can be fearful to challenge, either brushing over or even ignoring it because we don't want to lose a friend or be the bad guy.

If you are particularly fearful of these conversations, as I am, then here are a few tips for preparing yourself.

Remember where you came from. You did not always have your level of Christian maturity or understanding. You have probably struggled with, if not the exact same sin, something relatable. It may be something you have not dealt with for a long time, but don't be proud and judgmental, for that temptation can always sneak up on you again. If you can see the person you're speaking to in the same light as yourself – a sinner in need of correction and grace – you will be more loving, and more able to win them rather than accuse them.

Sharon says:

> As I challenge sin, I'm always questioning my own heart, asking, 'Do I struggle with this also?' This has encouraged me to keep short accounts and be honest about the state of my own heart, driving me back to Christ and His word. I always remind myself I have nothing but Christ to bring to the table and the encouragement to keep on keeping on.

Don't catastrophize. There is a certain amount of preparation you can bring to a conversation like this. It's good to review the Bible verses about the particular sin you're tackling, so you can answer the 'why' and 'where does it say' questions. But if you run the conversation over and over in your head beforehand, you're likely to come up with ever increasing disaster scenarios involving the loss of a friendship, the split of a church and the end of the world! You may even work yourself into such a level of anxiety that you will avoid having the conversation at all. Trust God. If He has called you to be a messenger in this instance, then you are simply part of His purposes. 'Do not be anxious beforehand what you are to say, but say whatever is given you in that hour, for it is not you who speak, but the Holy Spirit.'[3] Lean on His power, not your own powers of persuasion.

It's not about you. If someone chooses not to listen to you, you didn't 'lose'. That person is disobeying God, not you. You have been obedient. That is all you have to be. Do you want to be an enabler of sin or a good and faithful servant? A stumbling block, or one who points someone to the firm foundation? Now, where this gets hard is when you feel the need to speak to a child or new Christian who repeatedly won't listen to you and won't repent before God. At that stage, you may need to call in the reinforcements and ask your minister or elder for help in speaking to them, and maybe they can help you take a new approach (although this should only ever be done in the strictest confidence, as your spiritual child's sin is not fodder for gossip). Remember, you are still learning too!

Formal Discipleship

At Niddrie, the discipleship programme is based on a series of seventeen questions which cut right to the heart of a Christian's attitudes, actions and priorities. I'll reprint three of them in our question section below (along with a fourth,

---

3.   Mark 13:11. Here, the Lord is telling His disciples what mindset they should have when they are arrested and persecuted for believing in Him. I believe, however, that it is applicable to any difficult conversation we may have in His name – there is no circumstance in which Jesus tells us to be anxious or to over-prepare in our own wisdom!

of my own), but I'd deeply recommend obtaining the full list.[4] They are helpful for reflection even on your own, but when used for accountability in a discipling relationship, they are absolutely searing. In a good way that we all need – and in 20schemes, Christians of all maturity levels, from the minister on down, are expected to use them in order to guard against sin taking root. I've often wished I had someone to ask me these questions – while also feeling terrified of them! Sharon explains how she begins the discipleship process once a young Christian has agreed to a one-to-one relationship:

> I take the opportunity to explain the point, the purpose and why it's good for us. I explain what confidentiality means (we have a policy outlining it) and talk through some examples of when I may have to share what she has told me with the elders. I explain that our elders don't need to know every detail of every conversation, but if I'm concerned for her safety, the safety of others or if there is consistent, deliberate sinful behaviour and a refusal to repent that I will have no choice but to share out of concern for her spiritual and physical wellbeing. These conversations aren't as weird as you may think. In fact, outlining our purpose and confidentiality statement doesn't prevent women sharing but reminds them that our elders care and that confidentiality is taken seriously.
>
> Then I whip out the seventeen questions and we work through each one, explaining the purpose and why we are asking. Mostly this is filled with much laughter, especially with the questions that are a bit more intimate. After going through all this, no-one has ever said no and changed her

---

4. You can find the list in Sharon's book, or get it for free by signing up for the women's email list at 20schemes.com.

mind. Especially when I share my own personal struggle of first starting accountability. There isn't one person who isn't reluctant to share the blackness of their sinful heart with another – we all like our sin to stay hidden. But I, like all other women, have had to sit and decide for myself whether I really want my character to grow as a Christian. It's hard to be vulnerable with someone else, to trust them and share, but we must make a conscious choice to do it.

I explain that I'm weird: I always like to work backwards and start at question 17, because by the time I get to question one the answer will be a real one rather than the standard 'of course God's the most important thing in my life.' When we have sifted through all the questions, revealing the sinful responses and heart's desires at play, it's much harder to gloss over the most important question on the sheet with a trite answer.

I always ask, 'What question don't you want me to ask?', adding it to the list of questions, and usually finish by checking whatever I was keeping them accountable for last time.

We are often lazy Christians. We wriggle out of convicting Bible passages by deciding they don't apply to us in some way, or we have mitigating reasons why we can't be expected to live like that, or we

> *We wriggle out of convicting Bible passages by deciding they don't apply to us in some way.*

convince ourselves we don't really understand what the Lord is asking of us, or in especially hard-hearted times, we simply refuse to engage with them at all. We are good at rationalizing, even better at avoidance. In dry or busy times, we may just not examine ourselves in any detail for long seasons: no wonder we are so thankless and passionless before the Lord! It is much harder to fall into any of these attitudes if someone is challenging us on our persistent sin every couple of weeks. Hypocrisy becomes more of a challenge when we keep short accounts with the Lord!

Where do we see Jesus Discipling His Followers?

As Sharon points out, we see Jesus discipling His friends 24/7, taking them everywhere He goes, first winning their hearts, then teaching them doctrine, giving them an example to follow, correcting their sinful attitudes and their misconceptions about Him, and gradually increasing their responsibility.

One of the things my Bible teacher, Rabbi Cosmo, brought out in relation to the disciples that I have found helpful is their diversity. They were not a bunch of holy men Jesus plucked out of the pews of the local synagogue. Simon the Zealot was a Jewish nationalist who would have looked for the Messiah to deliver from the hated political oppression of Rome. Matthew was a tax collector who had probably colluded with Rome to take advantage of his own countrymen (that must have been a fun relationship for a while). James and John, the Sons of Thunder, wanted to call down lightning from heaven to smite their enemies; they were also ambitious for their own places, thinking that Christ's kingdom worked like an earthly one and they were going to be President and Prime Minister respectively. Peter was, well, a bit of a wild card, veering from brilliant perception with 'You are the Christ, the Son of the living God' to earning a 'Get behind me, Satan' in the space of a paragraph.[5] And then there was Judas Iscariot.

Discipleship is messy! Yet Jesus never lost His temper with them, never ghosted them because He was just too worn out with everything on His plate, never made them feel small. He forgave quickly and didn't dwell on what they'd done wrong, no matter how many times or often they did it, instead pointing them on to keep going, and keep growing. I think that forgiveness is my favourite picture of the Lord as teacher.

Think of Peter's frame of mind the week after Jesus' death. He was in absolute despair after denying he knew Christ. We may not know the intensity of Peter's regret, but we can probably taste it – that *I can't believe I did that, not when He was so good to me, not when I promised I'd be there for Him.* There is no cure for that kind of inner anguish, except forgiveness. What is the Lord's first conversation with Peter when He has risen? He gives him three opportunities to confess his love for Jesus, and on each occasion, not only does Jesus forgive him, He assures Peter that He has a plan and purpose for him. Not only is Peter to move on from his guilt, he is to 'feed my lambs'.[6]

How do we know this story? Surely because Peter told it and retold it to the blossoming Church. He lived out repentance and it changed him forever.

---

5.   Mark 8:27-33.

6.   John 21:15-17.

Verses on Discipleship

Wounds from a friend can be trusted [are faithful], but an enemy multiplies kisses (Prov. 27:6 NIV).

Perhaps you have been corrected by someone in your life who has helped you see yourself in a new way. It can be devastating to hear criticism initially, but if we let the Lord examine that area of our life, we can end up truly grateful to the person whom He used to speak to us.

A new commandment I give to you, that you love one another: just as I have loved you, you also are to love one another. By this all people will know that you are my disciples, if you have love for one another (John 13:34-35).

In the Old Testament, all of God's laws were summed up in the one great commandment 'Love the Lord your God ...and love your neighbour as yourself.' Here, Jesus is telling His followers to love one another more than themselves – to love them to the death! Following the letter of Moses' law did not always lead to sacrificial love. It could result in legalism and hypocrisy and looking down on those who were considered less righteous. Here Jesus is showing that keeping the spirit of the law – the law of love, which He kept perfectly and fulfilled in death – will be a testimony to His power. Such love will be irresistible to a watching world. Do you love those in your church so well that Christ Himself is evident to those around you?

Follow my example, as I follow the example of Christ (1 Cor. 11:1 NIV).

I wonder how many of us would dare to say to our younger Christian friends, 'Watch my spiritual life and do as I do!' We can only give them this example by keeping our eyes fixed on Jesus in every circumstance. There is a slight error in

> *In times of uncertainty, we should think 'What did Jesus do?'*

the old motto 'What would Jesus do?' – because that gives us a certain amount of latitude to imagine up godly responses for ourselves. Rather, in times of uncertainty, we should think 'What **did** Jesus do?' As we've discovered throughout this book, there is no major theme in our lives for which we cannot find an example of Christ's behaviour. Not even motherhood!

Questions

1. What has been more important to you than God in the last week?
2. Is there any sin that you've become aware of but love too much to repent of?
3. Have you been good and faithful with what God has given you in terms of time, money, and gifts?
4. How have you found delight and comfort in the Lord Jesus in the last week?

Song

Oh how good it is when the family of God
Dwell together in spirit, in love and unity;
Where the bonds of peace, of acceptance and love
Are the fruits of his presence here among us.

Oh how good it is to embrace his command
To prefer one another, forgive as he forgives.
When we live as one we all share in the love
Of the Son with the Father and the Spirit.
– 'Oh How Good It is', Stuart Townend

5. A Spiritual Mother through Hospitality

Sarah Edwards

Sarah Edwards is best known as the wife of Jonathan Edwards, the Colonial American revivalist who preached the famous sermon 'Sinners in the Hands of an Angry God'. It is often the case that, in the course of history, the legacy of women is preserved primarily because of their famous husbands or sons. In my previous book, *Ten Women Who Overcame Their Past*, I wrote about Sarah Edwards in her own right as a spiritual figure whose husband held her in the greatest respect. She experienced the Lord's presence in an almost tangible and certainly a dramatic way – a way that leaves us either sceptical or envious! Jonathan himself had no cynicism about Sarah's intense spiritual experiences, which included long trances in which she would meditate on Scripture and grasp the Lord's glory anew.

I suspect Jonathan had no difficulty in accepting Sarah's account of her inward revival because he saw the fruit of it in her life. An experience of the Lord should always leave us more holy, more loving, more passionate for souls, more like

Jesus Himself. And indeed, Sarah seems to have been only one example of a widespread revival in the Colonies at that time.

We are left an account by Samuel Hopkins, a Colonial preacher who lived with the family for a time, of Sarah's service within the home and relationships with her family. He was in fact living with them only a few weeks after Sarah's great spiritual renewal began, so he saw the fruits of it firsthand. Here is what he says of her as a mother:

> She had an excellent way of governing her children: she knew how to make them regard and obey her cheerfully without loud, angry words, or heavy blows. She seldom struck her children a blow; and in speaking to them used mild, gentle and pleasant words. If any correction was needful, it was not her manner to give it in a passion. And when she had occasion to reprove and rebuke, she would do it in few words, without heat and noise, with all calmness and gentleness of mind. And in her directions or reproofs, in any matters of importance, she would address herself to the reason of her children, that they might not only know her inclination and will, but at the same time, be convinced of the reasonableness of it.
>
> ... the chief care of forming children by government and instruction, naturally lies on mothers; as they are most with their children in their most pliable age, when they commonly receive impressions by which they are very much formed for life: so she was very careful to do her part in this important business. And when she met with any special difficulty in this matter, or foresaw any, she was wont to apply to Mr Edwards for advice and assistance: and on such occasions they would both attend to it, as a matter of great importance.

But this was not all, in which she expressed her care for her children. She thought that parents had great and important duty to do towards their children before they were capable of government and instruction. For them she constantly and earnestly prayed, and bore them on her heart before God, in all her secret and most solemn addresses to him; and that even before they were born. The evidence of her pregnancy, and consideration that it was with a rational, immortal creature, which came into existence in an undone, and infinitely dreadful state, was sufficient to lead her to bow before God daily for his blessing on it; even redemption, and eternal life by Jesus Christ. So that through all the pain, labour and sorrow, which attended her being the mother of children, she was in travail for them, that they might be born of God by having Christ formed in them.[1]

Hence Hopkins provides an overview of Sarah Edwards' character in a biography he wrote of Jonathan Edwards. But elsewhere, he focused in on Sarah's specific treatment of him:

When I arrived there, Mr Edwards was not at home, but I was received with great kindness by Mrs Edwards and the family and had encouragement that I might live there during the winter ... I was very gloomy and was most of the time retired in my chamber. After some days, Mrs Edwards came...

---

1. Jonathan Edwards and Samuel Hopkins. *The life and character of the late Reverend Mr Jonathan Edwards, president of the College at New-Jersey. Together with a number of his sermons on various important subjects.* (Northampton: Printed by Andrew Wright, for S. & E. Butler, 1804.). Unless otherwise noted, all citations in this chapter are from this volume. The entire text of Samuel Hopkins' biography of Jonathan Edwards, including a chapter on Sarah, can be found at https://quod.lib.umich.edu/e/evans/N07808.0001.001/1:13?rgn=div1;view=fulltext. Spelling and capitalization have been modernized for ease of reading.

and said as I was now become a member of the family for a season, she felt herself interested in my welfare and as she observed that I appeared gloomy and dejected, she hoped I would not think she intruded [by] her desiring to know and asking me what was the occasion of it ... I told her ... I was in a Christless, graceless state...upon which we entered into a free conversation and ... she told me that she had [prayed] respecting me since I had been in the family; that she trusted I should receive light and comfort and doubted not that God intended yet to do great things by me.

Sarah had seven children at the time – ages thirteen down to one and a half – and yet she also took this young man under her wing and encouraged him. He remembered it all his life.[2]

* * *

And whatever you do, in word or deed, do everything in the name of the Lord Jesus, giving thanks to God the Father through him (Col. 3:17).

After making much in our introduction about writing primarily about spiritual motherhood, you might wonder why I'm writing about a woman who had eleven children of her own. I am going to suggest, though, that we see those children as a backdrop. In the eighteenth century, large families were common (though all living to adulthood was an unusual blessing). Even with a mere three small children, I can't quite imagine living with Sarah's serenity! And it is worth

---

2. https://www.desiringgod.org/messages/sarah-edwards-jonathans-home-and-haven. This excellent blog post, by Noël Piper, is also a chapter in his book, *A God-Enhanced Vision of All Things*. Mr Piper quotes Samuel Hopkins here in Dodds, *Marriage to a Difficult Man*, p. 50.

noting how she treated her little ones: with respect, gentleness, patience, firmness, and constant prayer. If Sarah had just made that her life's work, running a calm and loving home for her busy husband and raising her enormous brood to know the

Just as not all biological mothers are 'spiritual' mothers, there are many mothers who have 'spiritual children' far beyond their own biological family.

Lord, that would have been a feat in itself. I would certainly settle for that legacy. But what I really want to discuss here is how Sarah treated those outside the family who came into her sphere. Just as not all biological mothers are 'spiritual' mothers, there are many mothers who have 'spiritual children' far beyond their own biological family.

Apart from the description of Sarah as a mother which we read above, Samuel Hopkins wrote about several other of her characteristics. Homing in on these will help us to see what specific attributes gave Sarah her peculiarly Christlike character.

Joy in Making a Happy Home

She paid proper deference to Mr Edwards, and treated him with decency and respect at all times.

... She accounted it her greatest glory, and that wherein she could best serve God and her generation, in being a means of promoting Mr Edwards's comfort and usefulness in this way. And no person of discerning could be conversant in the family without observing and admiring the great harmony and mutual love and esteem that subsisted between them.

When she herself laboured under bodily disorders and pains, which was often the case, she was not wont to be full of her complaints, and put on a dejected or sour countenance, being out of humour with everybody and everything, as if she was disregarded and neglected: but she would bare up under them with patience, and a kind of cheerfulness and good humour.

Whether or not our main sphere of work is inside our home, it's easy to go about our daily chores and employment with a sense of resentment. A recent poll showed that two-thirds of UK adults find their work unfulfilling. How many of us can say that we wake up looking forward to our day of work?

When you view your occupation or even your relationships with a sense of duty, they become a burden. Alternatively, viewing others' successes or family life with envy takes our focus off the Lord and hampers the process of our becoming like Him.

We can't always change our circumstances. We don't always get the job we want; we don't always get relief from the exhaustion or boredom or repetitiveness of our daily tasks. But can we learn to take joy in them?

Let's look for a moment at the well-known story of Mary and Martha in Luke 10:38-42:

Now as they went on their way, Jesus entered a village. And a woman named Martha welcomed him into her house. And she had a sister called Mary, who sat at the Lord's feet and listened to his teaching. But Martha was distracted by much serving. And she went up to him and said, 'Lord, do you not care that my sister has left me to serve alone? Tell her then to help me.' But the Lord answered her, 'Martha, Martha, you are anxious and troubled about many things, but one thing is necessary. Mary has chosen the good portion, which will not be taken away from her.'

Our common reading of this passage is that Martha is being petulant, and Jesus gives her a good telling-off. That is not quite how I see it. Jesus looks lovingly into her emotional state. He sees that she is someone who feels anxious and troubled, and is speaking out of 'the overflow of her heart'. Yes, He stands up for her sister's choices, but in that is also surely an invitation: that Martha is also free to choose the one necessary thing. After all, He is the One who came to free the anxious and troubled, and Martha too can find freedom in His presence. She has a serving nature, but through Him she can learn to serve out of gratitude and not anxiety.

Have you ever had the Lord speak to you as Jesus speaks to Martha here? A loving call of her name, an acknowledgment of her struggles, and a gentle rebuke to bring her priorities back into order. He teaches us so patiently!

Sarah Edwards did not have a prolific ministry like her husband. She was a servant to her household and all who entered it. But she had learned to 'sit at the Lord's feet' and put that first, and let all her service flow out of His ongoing presence and her joy in Him. Everyone who came close to Sarah saw Christ through her – because He too was a willing servant, who took care for those around Him more than for Himself.

While Jonathan Edwards was the family's spiritual leader, Sarah was its backbone. She ministered to the happiness of the whole home, to the relationships between the children, and enabled Jonathan's ministry.

How do we find joy in the Lord that can feed everything else we do? Surely through relationship and gratitude. Relationship with Christ can only thrive through regular Bible reading and prayer; and not in a perfunctory, dutiful way. Rather, we must seek the Lord's actual presence to feed us, give us peace, and transform our hearts and lives. Let's delight and rest in Him, not tick a box in our daily routine. Let's pour out our hearts before Him, whether that means confessing sin, crying out for help, or even offering up the staleness of our spiritual lives.

Relationship and gratitude go together. It is the gratitude that feeds our delight in Him. Gratitude for who He is (the Living One, perfect and holy and totally other from us, yet making Himself known), the example He gave us (humility, patience, utter lovingkindness, yet perfect righteousness), and what He has done (the Creator of all, the Giver of every good and perfect gift, God who dwelt among us, the Saviour who died for us and rose again). When we experience His presence, our gratitude grows more and more, because there is total joy and peace in that place. Sarah Edwards saw all that Christ had given and done for her, and all her work was a return of thanks.

Psalm 116:16 says, *O Lord, I am your servant ... you have loosed my bonds.* The Lord saves us from our captivity to sin, anxiety, and even duty, and with that freedom we receive the ability to serve Him willingly and joyfully. Saying that Christians should 'find joy in the Lord!' always sounds like a platitude to me. What I want to know is *exactly how* to find joy in the Lord. And the answer is to think of something for which to give thanks, and do it, and keep doing it.

Bringing Others into the Happy Home

In the course of reading about the lives of Christians who have gone before, you can't help but notice a 'family resemblance' between those who have served the Lord, albeit at different times and in different ways. Sarah Edwards has a kindred spirit in Betsie ten Boom, mentioned in my previous book, who, like her mother, ran an open home. The soup pot and the coffee pot were always ready for anyone who might come through the door, and frequent deliveries were made to any who were sick, poor or struggling throughout the town. Sarah served in a similar way:

> She was remarkable for her kindness to her friends and visitants, who resorted to Mr Edwards's. She would spare no pains to make them welcome, and provide for their convenience and comfort. And she was peculiarly kind to strangers, who came to her house. She would take such kind and special notice of such, and so soon get acquainted with them, as it were, and show such regard and concern for their comfort, and so kindly offer what she thought they needed, as to discover she knew the heart of a stranger, and well understood how to do it good; and so as to oblige them to feel in some measure as if they were at home.

Have you ever received this kind of welcome from someone outside your own family – someone who owes you nothing, and to whom you are perhaps even a stranger?

I can think of a number of times I have experienced this, but one recent occasion sticks in my mind. Someone in my family was having one of the frequent illnesses that accompanies life with small children, and I was more than usually hassled. I mentioned this to the women's leadership team at my church, just in passing, but said I was coping fine.

The next night, one of our ministers showed up at my front door with an enormous bag including a still-warm meal from his wife, pudding, snacks, and even books and little toys for the children. It was not just a church person dropping off a casserole – it was abundance. And for someone who was feeling lonely and overwhelmed, it was spiritual as well as physical food. It wasn't just the gift, or even the generous nature of it; it was the being seen.

> *Hospitality is caring for physical needs while also offering a sense of spiritual home.*

Not everyone is a cook or enjoys organising dinner parties! Yet, hospitality is a spiritual gift we can all practise. Hospitality is giving someone a lift home in the rain. Hospitality is sending a pizza order to a tired family. Hospitality is a care package to a missionary who is missing home comforts. Hospitality is caring for physical needs while also offering a sense of spiritual home. In doing so, we show people that we truly see them, that we care for them, and that we do so for Jesus' sake. It offers them nourishment and rest and an opportunity for gratitude, not just to us but to God.

My minister and his wife didn't wait to ask if I needed help (indeed, I think I had turned down an offer, out of a desire not to burden others and – let's be honest – to be seen as self-sufficient). Instead, they simply filled the need. So often, we employ the useful phrase, 'Just let me know if I can help' rather than just going ahead and helping. True, we need to have some knowledge of the people we're serving if we're going to do it effectively and tactfully; there is no use bringing a cake over to cheer someone up if we haven't taken the trouble to find out they're diabetic! The point is, we can't always wait for someone to ask for help, because often people don't. Let's give abundantly anyway: it's what God does, and we represent Him.

In serving others, whether inside our actual house or not, we extend to them our sense of home. By treating others like family, we bring them into ours. And there is no better way to allow people to be comfortable with us, even vulnerable, and open a door to show them Christ.

Extending her Happy Home into Stony Places

> She made it her rule to speak well of all, so far as she could with truth, and justice to herself and others. She was not wont to dwell with delight on the imperfections and failings of any; and when she heard persons speaking ill of others, she would say what she thought she could with truth and justice in their excuse ... She could bear injuries and reproach with great calmness & patience, without any disposition to

render evil for evil; but on the contrary, was ready to pity and forgive those who appeared to be her enemies.

Sarah Edwards experienced perhaps more than the usual amount of betrayal and injustice amongst her friends. Her husband instigated a considerable fracture in their town when he imposed a rule that church membership should be limited to those who had professed faith in Christ and taken communion (people had to be church members in order to hold leadership places in the town, so his decision provoked anger in those who did not confess Jesus). While Jonathan remained a popular preacher throughout New England, he became *persona non grata* to those in his own town, and so did Sarah by implication. She was deeply grieved by those friends and acquaintances who turned against them, even fought against them. Eventually, they had to leave their church.

Outside of her relationship with Christ, having the good opinion of her family and her town was Sarah's chief concern. Her greatest spiritual crisis came when she realised she had made an idol of this desire – and her greatest spiritual triumph came when Christ freed her from it, filling her longing for others' approval with longing for Himself instead. She came to be, for a time, entirely filled up with an experience of His presence.

Because Sarah was so complete in Christ, and so filled with the Holy Spirit, she was able to treat her enemies just as He had treated His: with compassion and forgiveness. There can be no doubt that she treated her false friends with the Bible's great recipe for revenge – *'If your enemy is hungry, give him bread to eat, and if he is thirsty, give him water to drink, for you will heap burning coals on his head ...*[3] – but that she did so not motivated by revenge, but by the desire to win even her enemies to a better experience of Christ.

If we can become resentful of our work, we can also certainly become bitter toward those who have wronged us. But neither of these are the Lord's way. And if we seek Him first, as Martha's sister Mary did, then they will not be our experience of life either. Instead, we will be centred in the 'home' of His presence, and we will be able to extend that sense of 'home' to those we meet, whether friends, foes or strangers.

Finding her Happy Home in Jesus' Presence

> She was eminent for her piety and experimental religion. Religious conversation was much her delight; and this she promoted in all companies as far as was proper and decent for her: and her discourse showed her understanding in divine things, and the great impression they had on her mind. The friends of true religion ... she would open her mind freely, and tell them the exercises of her own heart; and what God had done for her soul, for their encouragement, and excitement in the ways of God. Her mind appeared, to them who were most conversant with her, constantly to attend to divine things, even on all occasions, and in all business of life.

There is a temptation, when reading about a woman like Sarah Edwards, to think of her as a sort of different species of woman – one that we will never be. So much of Sarah's life sounds like

---

3.   Proverbs 25:21-22.

endless *doing*. So many things that we just don't feel we have inside us. So much efficiency and discipline and self-control and gentleness and goodness and – well, as I go on, my list starts to morph into the Fruit of the Spirit.

Surely that is Sarah Edwards' life. It was 'doing', as all of our lives are 'doing', but before all that came 'abiding'. From early childhood, Sarah's greatest interest was what it meant to be in relationship with Christ. All of the peace, joy, and patience she showed in her life were things she first received from much time with Him.

There is a school of thought that no one is really a prodigy. Sure, little Wolfgang was musically inclined and had a great ear for how music worked – but it was practice, hours and weeks and years of it, that turned him into the world's greatest composer. He could have wasted those years and turned out work as mediocre as his contemporaries, or given up music altogether. So with Sarah Edwards: her heart might have been inclined toward the Lord's things, but without many hours and years committed to Him, in repentance and seeking and constant prayer, His fruit would never have appeared in her life.

> *I have loved Jesus Christ since I was a child, but I spent most of those years trying to behave like Him – not to feel, think and desire like Him.*

If we have come to Christ, if we have experienced His call in our lives and committed to following Him, then we too have the inclination that first sparked in Sarah Edwards' childhood. We have an 'ear', as it were, for the Lord's song. It is in the continual seeking of the Lord that we experience

His presence more and more clearly, we rely on Him more, we gain a better understanding of His heart toward people (and toward us), and finally we start to reflect His desires, His attitudes and His character. I have loved Jesus Christ since I was a child, but I spent most of those years trying to behave like Him – not to feel, think and desire like Him.

Abiding in Christ *tells*. Why was Sarah Edwards such an effective servant of the Lord? She had surrendered all to Him. Hopkins writes that she had given up her own life and those of her relatives to Jesus, and was quite willing to submit to any trial that He might ordain – and that peace remained with her even when facing Jonathan's death, and facing her own.

Jesus gives us so many analogies in the Bible of what our relationship with Him should look like. In various passages we are sheep, children, servants, friends, heirs, a body, a bride, and more. This is perhaps to allow for the different perspectives we all bring to life. A single friend really made me think when she said she struggled with passages which compare our relationship to God with marriage or discuss Christian parenthood, because those things are hard for her to identify with.

This surprised me because I don't approach those same passages as a wife or a mother, but as alone before the Lord, and as a child rather than a parent. What really hits me hard, on the other hand, are the descriptions of God as a loving Father, and of the sense of home that we are headed for, because I left my parents at a young age and have struggled with terrible homesickness for so many years. The Lord knows how to speak into our individual hearts and to fire our longing for Him.

In the end, though, everyone desires love and a peaceful home. Those things can only be found ultimately in Him, because He is the source of love and peace. Remember the chapter on happiness: it is Him, not our desires, which truly give us contentment. Once we have found our home and our belonging in Him, we can extend that to others and bring them too into the family. Extend the tents. Throw open the doors!

Jesus' Example of Hospitality

We associate hosting and hospitality with food. In Jesus' case, this is often the breaking of bread. Whenever we see Him feeding people, it comes with prayer and the giving of thanks to His Father. But there is a much wider sense in which we see Jesus providing hospitality.

Jesus practised servanthood, and hosts do serve their guests – but they also have a sense of authority, welcoming people into a place that belongs to them, where they have the right to preside, to welcome, to offer refreshment but also to impose 'the rules of the house'. A good guest takes their shoes off if requested and uses the coaster provided!

In this respect Jesus really is, as the old saying says, 'the unseen host of every meal'. Not just for Christians, but for all; not just in church, but everywhere in His creation. We live in His world, where He requests us to follow His house rules and provides abundantly for everything we might require during our stay here. We all enjoy His hospitality, though most do not take full advantage of their host's wonderful company. Jesus explains His version of hospitality in His own words:

> *Therefore I tell you, do not be anxious about your life, what you will eat or what you will drink, nor about your body, what you will put on. Is not life more than food, and the body more than clothing? Look at the birds of the air: they neither sow nor reap nor gather into barns, and yet your heavenly Father feeds them. Are you not of more value than they?*
>
> *And which of you by being anxious can add a single hour to his span of life? And why are you anxious about clothing? Consider the lilies of the field, how they grow: they neither toil nor spin, yet I tell you, even Solomon in all his glory was not arrayed like one of these. But if God so clothes the grass of the field, which today is alive and tomorrow is thrown in the oven, will he not much more clothe you, O you of little faith?* (Matt. 6:25-30).

The world is His. Not only the cattle on a thousand hills, but the flour in a thousand supermarkets, the oil in a thousand cargo ships and the milk in a thousand dairies, to relate to our production-line culture! The sinful world does not always work as He originally

Music, flowers, spices, laughter, sex, animal life, seasons, creativity are all His gifts to us. And they are very good.

designed. Famines fall upon a land which we cursed with sin. People impose hunger and want on each other for the sake of their own power or greed. Yet God Himself provides and watches over all His creation, and He mitigates more of our suffering than we will ever know. He lavishes us not only with what we need but with beauty and variety and pleasure. Music, flowers, spices, laughter, sex, animal life, seasons, creativity are all His gifts to us. And they are very good. The best host, He really has thought of everything!

One more thing. Like the manna God fed to His people in the wilderness, we need His feeding every day. We need prayer, trust, His Word, hope and reliance anew every morning. Don't go hungry for no reason, and don't selfishly take His provision without giving thanks. A good host is only truly appreciated by a good guest.

Verses on Hospitality

Behold, I stand at the door and knock. If anyone hears my voice and opens the door, I will come in to him and eat with him, and he with me ... Go therefore to the main roads and invite to the wedding feast as many as you find (Rev. 3:20, Matt. 22:9).

> *You can't say you 'just don't feel called', because He has made it clear He is calling anyone who will come with an open heart.*

Jesus gave to John, to pass on to us, an explicit invitation. If you have read Revelation 3:20 (and you just have!), then this means you. There is no excuse for passing by Jesus' door; He has answered every objection. You can't be too poor, because He has welcomed the poor in spirit. You can't be too unworthy, because He has offered forgiveness and transformation. You can't say you 'just don't feel called', because He has made it clear He is calling anyone who will come with an open heart. If you don't know how to answer Jesus' knock, ask the most loving Christian you know. And if you don't know any, come to my blog and ask me!

Everyone welcome, all you can eat.

For the majority of you reading this who already know Jesus' fellowship and leading, He gives another explicit command. You are not to come to the feast alone if you can help it. Invite everyone you know. Everyone welcome, all you can eat. If Christ is the host, we are the waiters – His hands and feet, serving everyone around us with the goal of bringing food to all the spiritually starving.

Hope, love, peace. We need this daily bread every single day. We all need it, even those who don't realise it yet. For, when they taste and see that the Lord is good, like a delicious hors d'oeuvre, it will whet their appetite for the full meal.

> *Ho! Everyone who thirsts, come to the waters; and you who have no money, come, buy and eat. Yes, come, buy wine and milk without money and without price. Why do you spend money for what is not bread, and your wages for what does not satisfy? Listen carefully to Me, and eat what is good, and let your soul delight itself in abundance* (Isa. 55:1-2 NKJV).

This is the invitation of God to His unfaithful people as their exile is imminent, but imagine Jesus calling it out in the marketplace. I just had to include that 'Ho!' from the King James – in other translations it says 'Come,' or 'Behold,' or 'Hey,' or even 'You there!' Jesus wants our attention. He wants with all His being to give us freely the only thing that can ever satisfy our deepest desire. We often feel awkward about accepting things for free, especially expensive things. It's almost funny how He addresses that need to feel like we are contributing something. 'Come and buy' – but He doesn't take money! What does this host want from us? He wants us to accept His hospitality, and to enjoy our company, and to bring us into a feast that will never end.

Who is to come? The thirsty. You can't come to this feast feeling already full. It's like showing up to Christmas dinner after filling up on tinned soup and toast. You have no appetite, you're stuffed by what you ate but didn't really enjoy it; it doesn't feel like a celebration, and you have no interest in sitting there in everyone else's company as they eat. You get no benefit from that dinner whatsoever. Don't fill up on what the world has to offer and think you're satisfied. Take your needs and your longing to Christ, and enjoy the company which both He and His Church offer, and feast on His presence and promises.

Questions

1. What would you like others to experience when they come into your home?
2. How can you extend that sense of home out into the community?
3. What can you give thanks for that will help feed your sense of willing servanthood through gratitude?

And He walks with me and He talks with me
And He tells me I am His own
And the joy we share as we tarry there
None other has ever known.
– 'In the Garden', C. Austin Miles

6. A Mother with Special Challenges

Emily Colson

Emily Colson is the daughter of Chuck Colson, the Watergate lawyer who found Christ in prison and turned evangelist. Her early life was full as she travelled between her divorced parents, both of whom were loving and generous, although her father was preoccupied with his own career. In her teens, Emily experienced a massive shock when Chuck was implicated in the scandal of President Nixon's wire-tapping of the Democratic National Headquarters, and subsequently sentenced to prison.

Her life was turned upside-down more gradually by Chuck Colson's profession of faith after a friend shared Christ with him around the time of his sentencing. Seeing the change in her father's heart and demeanour, Emily was drawn more and more to the freedom he had found in Jesus.

In the meantime, however, she had grown up, graduated from university, and built a career as an artist. She was sophisticated, well-travelled, part of a famous family; she was one of the cultural elite, and she loved life.

When Chuck was kept in hospital following a complicated surgery for cancer, Emily flew to him and barely left his side for weeks. It was in those weeks that she came to truly know her father on a deeper level – but there was a consequence for this time she had with him. Existing tensions with her husband were exacerbated by her absence, and he left; however, after some months of separation, they reconnected and came back together.

If you've noticed a pattern of Emily's life undergoing major changes due to the circumstances of those around her, the biggest shifts were yet to come, almost together. First, Max was born: Emily's much-wanted baby, who showed very early signs of severe autism. Eighteen months later, with a sense that she no longer had time or attention for him, Emily's husband left. Finally, and wrapped up in these new challenges, Emily made a rock-solid commitment to following Jesus and joined a church.

From this point on, Emily's main occupation was as Max's full-time carer. She had the support of her church, her family (who lived far away) and most of all her God, but still the exhaustion was all-encompassing:

> At the end of the day it's just Max and me. And this thing called autism ... Max is not a burden; he is my greatest gift. I'm not about to give up. I'm just not sure I can keep going.
>
> 'Do you see this, God? I know you're watching. I know you're in this, but we're at a dead end ... Why would you bring us this far, sustain us, provide for us, carry us through a

war zone, if it was only to end here – a place without hope? I don't even know what to pray for anymore.'[1]

This is where Emily's story of motherhood begins: with a sense, yes, of blessing, but also of helplessness and all-encompassing need. All of her reliance had to be on the Lord. Yet her story is not ultimately one of weariness, but of great beauty and victory, and it gives tremendous hope to others who are feeling worn down by caring for high-dependence loved ones. If you only read one of the books I recommend, please let it be this one. It will feed the soul of anyone who is a carer for children or vulnerable adults.

Instead of placing all of Emily's story together chronologically, we're going to look at several different aspects of her motherhood of Max in her own words.

* * *

In the multitude of my anxieties within me, Your comforts delight my soul (Ps. 94:19 NKJV)

Emily's Walk with Jesus

One night I threw myself over the end of my bed, hollow, shattered, and began to pray. And the most unexpected thing happened. I got an answer. I knew it was God because he told me something so contrary to my own thoughts, and so distressing that I immediately stopped praying and threw my eyes open.

Jesus wanted me to take his hand and walk with him.

---

1.   Emily Colson, *Dancing with Max: A Mother and Son who Broke Free,* (Zondervan: Grand Rapids, 2010), pp 28-30.

It was beautiful and startling and breathtaking. At the same time, I wanted him to have some sort of magic wand to poof my life back to perfect. What I had prayed was for my precious child to be with me, for him to be safe and well. I prayed for a home and finances and food and work and friends and hope.

... 'Okay,' my willing heart quickly responded. 'I'll have to get Max first.' And this is where it all fell apart. It was his response to me, so contrary to my instincts, that sent me into a panic. 'I'll take him later,' he told me ... Jesus had a hand, and a plan, for each of us.[2]

Have you ever been in a situation where you were concerned for someone, and every time you listened to a sermon or read a Bible passage you thought *That person really needs this message!* I'm sure there are times when a particular sermon might well be relevant to the friend on your mind – but if you're constantly focused on someone else's spiritual need, then there's a good chance you need to open your own ears to what God is saying. He wants to seek your heart, too. He wants you to be repentant, and renewed, and secure, and free. Your identity is not 'someone's carer'. Your identity is 'child of God'. There is only resentment and exhaustion to be had out of serving Him of your own strength, even your own will.

> *If you're constantly focused on someone else's spiritual need, then there's a good chance you need to open your own ears to what God is saying.*

---

2.   Colson, *Dancing with Max,* pp. 100-101.

If you feel pretty secure in your Christian life (even, I might suggest, taking it for granted) then the harder part of trust, for you, might not be trusting that God has a good plan for your life, but also a good plan for other people's lives. Trusting that He can still reach your children who have not yet come to Him. Trusting that He will convict of sin where it is needed, and that your job is not to convince someone they're wrong but patiently to forgive where you have been wronged. Trusting that He can use people that seem to you almost useless. Trusting that He can heal bodies, and hearts, and relationships.

When you can trust God for the people that you love (and, just as hard, the people that you DON'T love!) then you can have enough mental and emotional space to seek Him yourself and listen to what He says through His Word. Can you give over to Jesus your anxious cares for other people in order to find rest in Him? 'Cast all your anxiety on Him, because He cares for you.'[3]

Loving like Jesus

Emily describes a stressful meeting – one of so many – where she had taken Max for assessment by a panel of experts. As she sits with her child, listening to them talk about all his challenges and limitations, she is simply overcome with love for him and draws him into a hug:

> ... this is grace, the help I needed, the gift I can't survive
> without: a beautiful, unexpected, inexplicably perfect love

---

3.   1 Peter 5:7 (BSB).

raining down upon us even in the midst of the darkest moments.

'What a big day you've had, Maxi,' I whispered into his ear. 'You did a great job.' I could hear oohs and ahs from the four evaluators, as if love and grace lapped over the sides, spilling onto them and soaking all their notes.

When we live as though the people we care for are precious to us, it changes other people's perceptions. It opens the outside world's eyes to the value and the God-imaging beauty of those whom they would ordinarily overlook or dismiss. By taking that moment to relish her son in a stressful environment, Emily gained an experience of true joy, but she also showed Max how loved and wonderful she thought he was, and she pointed the experts to a love that reached deeper than all the labels and strategies they used to define her son.

To look at it from another angle – if, instead of resting in our love for the spiritual children God has given us, we treat them as a nuisance, or too demanding, or inferior, then that also translates into the way they see themselves, and the way the outside world sees them. If we dishonour those God loves, then we dishonour Him. If we focus on the demanding and disappointing areas of pastoral care, then we lose the joy that comes with the privilege of ministry; and with that attitude, we are unlikely to bear any fruit from that relationship. Encouragement and, yes, enjoyment of our spiritual children is important.

Raising three small children as a stay-at-home mom has sometimes felt like drowning. Yet, on every trip to our local park, no matter how irritating or disobedient or demanding

I might have found a kid at some point in the day, I watch them running through the forest path on their way home with a smile – grateful not just because we are on our way home (!) but because these are gifts God has lent to me, and someday I will be sad when no little legs are flying down that path. Gratitude is something God is gradually growing in me.

Emily had to learn to reflect God's love not only for Max, but also for his father, who had left her in such a desperate situation. One night, on a visit to her father, he heard her saying prayers with Max. Later that evening, he reproved her: 'You need to pray for Garry.' Emily was initially defensive, but eventually she knew he was right. '... I didn't realize until later the power of his advice that praying for someone else lets us see a ray of God's immense love for them, and some of that light spills back onto us.'[4]

Just like loving Max when the path could be so exhausting, Emily understood that loving the ex-husband who hurt her was actually for her good. Our love for others is only a dim reflection of the love and value that God places on them – a sacrificial love. Sometimes the sacrifice that we make, in reflecting our Father, is that of forgiveness. Forgiveness never makes us weak. In fact, it knocks over our image of people who have wronged us as huge, stone-like barriers, and allows us to see that they too are vulnerable, sometimes through the anger and callousness they have showed us. They are in need of Jesus' grace, just as we were, and just as we still are. Through praying for Garry, Emily was able to see him again as a man,

---

4.   Colson, *Dancing with Max*, p. 156.

not a thing. And rather than forgiveness brewing resentment in her, it gave her peace.

A woman who grows in Christlikeness shines like a light to other people too. Many mothers would have treated a severely autistic child like a burden. Instead, as Chuck Colson writes, her genuine love for Max is a testimony to a dark and selfish world:

> 'Whenever she has heard me call her 'heroic,' she cringes. 'No! No,' she says. 'It is a blessing!' I've discovered she really means it.
>
> The only possible explanation is that God's grace has poured through Emily, enabling her to give love selflessly. Her devotion is the kind that Jesus spoke of when he said, 'Greater love has no one than this, that he lay down his life for his friends' (John 15:13).'[5]

Max's Faith

Emily spoke often of Jesus to Max and prayed with him every day; they visited church in person when Max could tolerate it and watched videos of services when he couldn't. But Emily was never quite sure whether or not Max was capable of truly understanding or committing to the Lord's call. Her prayer for him, by the time he was in his early teens, was full of that 'trusting God's plan for other people' that we discussed earlier:

> If Max doesn't have the ability to express his faith, Lord, then please choose Max as if he had. But if he is able to understand, then I pray he'll accept you, even if he's never able to voice it.[6]

---

5. Ibid, p. 195.
6. Ibid, pp. 149-151.

God answered Emily beyond her expectations, and when he was fourteen Max asked if he could be baptised – specifically, in his grandfather's swimming pool, since he was easily overwhelmed by busy social settings. Emily and Chuck were dumbfounded by this request. They spent weeks quizzing Max to see if he truly understood salvation and baptism and the core tenets of faith. He was unmoving in his resolve: he wanted to identify with Jesus and be part of His community. In the end, there was no question that permitting him to be baptised was not only right, but invaluable for him. Emily writes:

> ... In that glistening water I saw every report that stamped Max insufficient, every rejection he has endured, every label the world had stuck to Max's broken places. It all washed away.[7]

Chuck adds:

> Max's expression was one of total and joyous acceptance. His countenance displayed the simple, childlike faith Jesus spoke of (Matt. 18:4).[8]

So often we are the ones sticking labels to people. *Autistic. Severely disabled. Learning difficulties. Addict. Mental illness.* Even *sinful.* We create barriers in our minds where Christianity becomes not quite off-limits, but hedged round with qualifications. This is what makes Emily's simple prayer so beautiful. She didn't know if Max could believe in the way

---

7.   Ibid.

8.   Ibid, pp.190-191.

the Bible tells us to believe, so she left Him in God's hands and trusted Him to be faithful and gracious.

Yet, when Max did make a profession, both she and her father wanted to make sure that his faith met their standards. Now, of course we must examine new believers to see if they truly understand both the salvation they are receiving and the lifelong commitment they are making. (I'm also in favour of encouraging children to wait to join the church until they are older teenagers, having seen too many join without a real understanding and then fall away later in life.) But can we sometimes use this to conform young Christians to our expectations of what that should look like?

I think what true faith comes down to is experience, trust and willingness: experience of God's goodness and loveliness, trust that He can save, and willingness to live in His strength. For young children and vulnerable adults, knowledge of God may come through knowing His people instead of reading the Bible for themselves. A young child may not be able to take in large sections of Scripture or heavy theology, but kindness and joy and an obvious love of the Lord will speak into any open heart. And the Lord delights in those who will trust Him totally and in all simplicity, walking with Him as with a beloved father. As Emily's pastor told her, 'The Holy Spirit speaks his language.'

Max has proved himself a true Christian in his readiness to share Jesus. He is unembarrassed to tell where his joy comes from. He loves to sing and worship in the back of the church and to serve by vacuuming the building each week. And he loves to pray, bringing Jesus' presence with him wherever he goes:

> Now each week after bowling we sit in the same sandwich shop together, in the same booth, and share a meal as friends. Max is still the first to hold out his hands to pray, but we all quickly follow. And each week prayer is an open conversation, as if Jesus were sitting at the table with us, completing our circle of communion, and holding ketchup-covered hands.[9]

Ministering to Others – Max and Emily

I recently read a list of 'helpful thoughts' that one of the ministers in my denomination had written for our magazine. There were quite a few that I found thought-provoking, and one of them was this: You can still serve even if your own need is greater.

> *You can still serve even if your own need is greater.*

Just because you are overwhelmed or struggling financially or fighting depression or illness, it doesn't mean God has nothing for you to do. Part of the joy of Christian life is the joy of giving to others, and thus giving to God. We are not bound by our own limitations. We have His strength when we are weak, His riches when we are poor, His shepherding when we are busy and resentful, His sustaining love when we are out of patience and energy. If we keep our eyes fixed on Him, we will still want to do what little we can to point others to the One who loves our soul, and bring Him glory. To serve in the midst of our own need is nothing but the power of God. We can

---

9. Ibid, p. 170.

get so caught up staring into the depths of our own suffering! Look up. Look up physically to the sky, and remember the goodness of the Creator. Look up and see others, and their places of need.

Look up.

When Max was a young schoolboy, Emily took a few days' mission trip to Peru with her father. She learned that most autistic children there never survive infancy. And she realised how full of blessing her exhausting life was: she still had the son that filled her with joy.

After she came home, Emily went through all of Max's lovingly preserved baby and toddler clothes, reliving all the memories, and then ironed a tiny label in each one: *Jesus me ama*, 'Jesus loves me'. It was a sacrifice to let go of these long unused clothes. They were memorials of her love for Max, of the time before his autism defined them both. Yet using them in an act of service, unimaginably, gave Emily not grief but joy:

> I tried to picture the children in Peru, with their black hair and coffee skin peeking out of Max's familiar clothing. I had always dreamed I would have more children to fill them. And indeed, I do. I hesitated before I taped the last box and couldn't help but open it one more time to soak in the memories of my sweet Max. What I saw instead was a label. *Jesus me ama.*[10]

We are all needy children before the Lord. We all must rely on Him to the extent that anything we do *for* Him is really

---

10. Ibid, pp. 86-87.

done *through* Him. In all the demands and wearinesses and resentments that dog us, we still have the comfort of His presence, forgiveness, leading. Our physical needs are not greater than the spiritual needs of the world around us. We have all things through Christ.[11]

How does Jesus Minister to the Vulnerable?

The wonderful thing is that Jesus wants us all to be as vulnerable, trusting, and full of wonder as Max. He just loves seeing those things in us. We all know that He said, 'Suffer the little children to come unto me', but He also said that we must all be like little children.[12] And it's not just in the person of Jesus that we see this compassion; the Old Testament, that volume supposedly full of violence and harshness, speaks constantly of God's care for the vulnerable, represented by the orphan, the immigrant and the widow. Jesus reached out to the socially unacceptable tax collectors and prostitutes, the ethnically hated Samaritans, the difficult-to-be-around, like Zacchaeus, the demon-possessed, even the Roman occupiers. He ministers to those we write off, and He does great things through them.

He ministers to those we write off, and He does great things through them.

In Luke 10, the Lord sends seventy disciples to preach, heal and cast out demons in His name. When they return, amazed

---

11. It bears reading in full – '*He who did not spare his own Son but gave him up for us all, how will he not also with him graciously give us all things?*' (Rom. 8:32).

12. Luke 18:17.

at their newfound power, He shares their joy, yet in a way that will not puff up any sense of pride.

> *Nevertheless, do not rejoice in this, that the spirits are subject to you, but rejoice that your names are written in heaven.*
>
> *In that same hour he rejoiced in the Holy Spirit and said, 'I thank you, Father, Lord of heaven and earth, that you have hidden these things from the wise and understanding and revealed them to little children; yes, Father, for such was your gracious will.'*[13]

He can do His greatest work through those who empty themselves and place all of their trust in Him.

Verses

> *Though the Lord is exalted, he looks after the lowly, and from far away humbles the proud* (Ps. 138:6 NET).

Which would you rather be? Let's not judge others' capacity to know and be used by Jesus, lest we be humbled by Him.

> *At that time the disciples came to Jesus, saying, 'Who is the greatest in the kingdom of heaven?' And calling to him a child, he put him in the midst of them and said, 'Truly, I say to you, unless you turn and become like children, you will never enter the kingdom of heaven. Whoever humbles himself like this child is the greatest in the kingdom of heaven.'*
>
> *'Whoever receives one such child in my name receives me, but whoever causes one of these little ones who believe in me to sin, it would be better for him to have a great millstone fastened*

---

13. Luke 10:20-21.

around his neck and to be drowned in the depth of the sea
(Matt. 18:1-6).

God not only deeply values the innocence and safety of His
little ones, He is fiercely protective of them. This has two
consequences for us. One, if we are involved in mentoring
or nurturing a child or vulnerable adult, we have a grave
responsibility. How we treat people day by day, in small
interactions and large decisions and in our personal example,
has eternal consequences.

Second, if you are His child, then know that when you
have been abused and hurt, God is fierce in His protection
of you too. *'As a father shows compassion to his children, so
the Lord shows compassion to those who fear him.'*[14]

> *... a bruised reed he will not break, and a faintly burning
> wick he will not quench; he will faithfully bring forth justice*
> (Isa. 42:3).

We often take this verse to refer to Christians who are
smouldering, rather than burning, during times of hurt or
discouragement or coldness. But the passage is speaking of the
tenderness and humility of the great Servant of the Lord –
a king whose strength is in gentleness. He carefully tends to
all who are struggling, weak or disadvantaged, and He makes
bruised reeds into oaks of righteousness and smouldering
wicks into bright lights!

---

14. Psalm 103:13.

Questions

1. Who in your life are you tempted to 'write off' as being incapable, limited or undeserving of serving the Lord? How might your attitude toward them affect your care of them?

2. What are some ways you can grow gratitude for people you find tiring or demanding? Are there certain habits or traits you enjoy in them? Give thanks for the hard things too, recognising God's willingness to use these things to work in your own character.

3. What do you feel is limiting you in serving the Lord? What would motivate you to point others to Him, and what opportunities do you have to do so?

Song

This is one of my favourites. I sing it to my children. I sing it on my own as personal worship. It contains everything I need to get through the day:

Oh, how I love Jesus
Oh, how I love Jesus
Oh, how I love Jesus
Because He first loved me.

7. Mothering the Mothers

Patti

One of the threads that ran through *Dancing with Max* was the absolute necessity of a support network, especially for a mother of a child with particularly intensive needs. Throughout her life, Emily found this in different places: initially with her husband, then with her family (though they all lived far away and their support came in bursts), even from strangers, often those who had other autistic children in their lives. But the real day-to-day emotional and practical help came mostly from women in the local church. And that is how it's meant to be.

* * *

Older women likewise are to be reverent in behavior, not slanderers or slaves to much wine. They are to teach what is good, and so train the young women to love their husbands and children, to be self-controlled, pure, working at home, kind, and submissive to their own husbands, that the word of God may not be reviled (Titus 2:3-5).

Here the passage talks about both exampling godly behaviour and intentionally teaching and training younger women. This is closely connected to both Mentoring and Hospitality as already discussed, but here we will focus on stepping in as a support for those who are going through a particular challenge. As with our previous chapter, we'll go through Emily's experiences as we move through the topic. While the Christian friend who had the greatest impact on her life was Patti, a wonderful exemplar of warmth and kindness, Patti is also representative of the way whole communities of women rally round each other. We will look at her ministry alongside other women who came around Emily.

People who Step Up or Step Away

Emily describes a glamorous, civilized scene: an evening at her father's house with a small dinner party, hors d'oeuvres and sparkling water and real conversation. It lasted, for her, only a few minutes, until Max became overwhelmed and had to be taken away. She spent the rest of the party playing with him alone in another room:

> Wasn't anyone missing us? I felt I'd been assigned to the wobbly little aluminium children's table in the kitchen, while all the fancy guests enjoyed the real party. Aching with loneliness, I could hear them starting to say their good-byes. But before they left I overheard the man say, 'Emily is so filled with grace. You can just see it in her.'
> Grace? Was that my consolation prize? If this man could see grace, how did he miss seeing my enormous swirling turmoil? It made me furious – and jealous of their seemingly

perfect lives. I didn't need velvet-covered clichés. I needed love and comfort. I needed help.[1]

Even years on from this episode, when Emily had undoubtedly grown in the grace that people noticed in her even then, you can feel the memory of how her spirit cried out for help, for rest. These were Christian people who chose to enjoy their civilised evening, in the comforting thought that a mother was 'coping well', rather than minister to someone who was clearly left out and living an exhausting life.

Contrast this Christian dinner party with Emily's experience some years later of Mrs Woods. This was a stranger, a lady drawn into Max's life because of his obsession with a certain model of car. He wanted to explore her vehicle, and this lady took his unusual personality in her stride and let him and Emily into her life:

My son looked as if he'd just found the twin brother he'd searched for all his life. Mrs Woods never asked about Max's disability. She never gave me the 'aren't you wonderful' look, as if raising my son were a social cause rather than a love story.[2]

There are Christians who are kinder and more empathetic than non-Christians. We are all made in the image of God, enjoy His common grace and show aspects of His character. As Christians, surely we should aim to out-love and out-serve the world around us, but that is not always the case. This non-believing lady treated Emily and her son as ordinary people

1.   Colson, pp. 56-57.
2.   Colson, p. 142.

– which they are, in the context of their own lives – and saw Max as a beloved son, not as a burden. There is a complacency to the remark of the man at the dinner party. Because Emily seemed to be bearing up well under what he saw as a demanding situation, or even a ministry, he was content to praise her. But Mrs Woods saw instead an opportunity: a family that wanted to be part of her life, and a mother to whom she could show grace. Not everyone would allow an excited autistic teenager to explore their car regularly for an hour at a time. But she actively invited Max to enjoy it, without making Emily feel there was anything burdensome or even unusual in that.

It goes without saying that we should all aim to be Mrs Woods in this comparison: preferably without patting ourselves on the back afterward and telling everyone we know how heroic we are. We are only servants of the King, and we are no better than any others of the humans He made and so graciously rules over. If we can serve with our time, or our attention, or our help, or our money, that is no more than we owe: our 'reasonable service'. Emily mentions time and time again ordinary people who helped her restrain Max during an uncontrollable episode, or who showed good humour with his eccentric interests, or who simply spoke kindly in the grocery store instead of avoiding eye contact.

> *If we can serve with our time, or our attention, or our help, or our money, that is no more than we owe: our 'reasonable service'.*

The other question we need to ask is this: when you are in the mother's position (or carer, or mentor, or friend), are you willing to ask for, or even accept, help? Are you willing to ask for advice when you don't know how to handle a decision or a conflict with your spiritual children? Are you willing to show your

Are you willing to ask for, or even accept, help?

vulnerability and lay down your pride to say you can't cope as well as people think you can? To look for support and company when you are discouraged? To tell your spouse or ministry partner or your own mentor you are in need of extra prayer or a break or someone to spend time with your child alongside you?

Mothers cannot expect other people to be mind-readers. And yet the community around mothers needs to practice anticipating needs. Both of these are part of the 'dance' we learn in the community of Christ. Just as He truly sees us, we must have our spiritual eyes open to really see one another.

The Tongue of the Learned

Despite the rejection and exhaustion of divorce, one of the recurring themes in Emily's book is the friends, especially female friends, that stepped up to support her. She describes the first social occasion after her husband left the family home:

> Heather looked closely at my face, perfectly made-up to hide my swollen eyes. I had to say it, to release the truth before it shattered me.
>
> 'Garry left four days ago. He walked out. I don't know where he is.' The women rushed around me as if I'd been sprayed with shards of glass. I didn't want these women to see my pain, these mothers who were doing everything right,

who had husbands that stayed with them. But I didn't have the strength to hide. I let these women with the seemingly perfect lives see my frailty ... And in return they fed me warm blueberry cake and comforted me like a young child.[3]

Cathy, a woman I'd met at church and barely knew, hired a baby-sitter one day and came with me into court so that I wouldn't be alone. She didn't know anything about divorce law, but I felt bigger with her beside me.[4]

The women in these [Bible study] groups became my help line, my scaffolding. There were times when I arrived feeling desperate and fragile, with the emotional state of paper-thin porcelain. These women would gather around me in a circle, love me, pray over me with their hands stretched out like the lush green umbrella of the rain forest, bringing me back to life.[5]

What these women *didn't* have was specialist training with autistic kids, or an appropriate ministry platform, qualifications in counselling, or (in Cathy's case!) a law degree. All of these things are

> *Don't feel you need to have some kind of special background to serve someone with special needs.*

wonderful, even essential in their own circumstances, but don't feel you need to have some kind of special background to serve someone with special needs. Love is universal. As Max's pastor said that 'the Holy Spirit speaks Max's language,' make

---

3.   Ibid, pp. 49-50.
4.   Ibid, p. 51.
5.   Ibid, p. 90.

sure that He speaks your language too. Cake (or any kind of practical provision) and prayer and a listening ear are some of the greatest ministry tools. Don't overlook your spiritual gifts by placing an over-importance on your education and abilities. Jesus and His disciples were notable in their time for their lack of formal training. What they did was minister to people's hearts in whatever condition they found them.

So what do you do if a friend bursts into tears in front of you?

Do stick with her. Seeing people's vulnerability can make us uncomfortable. There is a temptation to look away or change the subject. A friend sharing her vulnerability opens up a path to you showing your vulnerability. Don't be afraid of that – the Lord uses these moments of honesty both for the speaker and the listener.

Don't feel the need to give loads of advice. Sitting quietly and allowing yourself to feel empathy is what Job's comforters did right! When they started grasping for solutions in their own strength is when they offended both Job and the Lord. That doesn't mean you can never offer help or insight or even constructive criticism, but make sure first that it's helpful and hopeful, and maybe even wait for the emotions to die down before having another conversation.

Do follow up. Text that you're praying about the issue a few days later; ask about it in a quiet moment at church. Chances are, if a woman is feeling distressed enough to cry in front of a friend, it's probably a big issue in her life and you're not going to upset her by bringing it up again. It is so comforting to know that someone is praying for you in an ongoing issue

– like they're doing some of the heavy emotional lifting alongside you.

Don't worry if you don't get too much detail about the problem. There are times when a woman won't say very much about something clearly upsetting her, for a variety of reasons. She's still working through her own feelings; she doesn't want to breach something confidential; she's ashamed of something that has happened. Give an opportunity to open up, and if she feels uncomfortable after a certain point, leave it there (unless you feel she is in danger). Do not press her for more out of your own curiosity, and certainly don't make her troubles an opportunity for gossip with others!

Do help practically – bring round a meal, buy a coffee, have a helpful book delivered. Instead of saying, 'Let me know if I can help,' ask 'What can I do to help?' And if she is noncommittal, as people often are, help anyway. Dropping off a plate of scones or a toy for the child is tangible love.

Help anyway.

Isaiah 50:4 describes this characteristic of the Servant of the Lord (Messiah):

> *The Lord GOD has given Me the tongue of the learned, that I should know how to speak a word in season to him who is weary. He awakens Me morning by morning, He awakens My ear to hear as the learned.*[6]

There are people with degrees and academic understanding who lack in empathy and generosity toward others. Jesus

---

6.   NKJV.

shows here our pattern of a truly erudite Christian: someone who hears others' needs and weariness, who hears what the Father would say to that person, and who graciously speaks comfort into their life.

True Friendship

It was at church that Emily met her greatest cheerleader, affectionately dubbed 'Peppermint Patti' by the Snoopy-loving Max. Patti, who had worked with autistic children in the past, had invited Max and Emily into her home and family straightaway when they met, and became their great emotional support. She was the first one to tell Emily, and frequently remind her, that Max was *a gift:*

> Thereafter Patti was on speed dial when I needed an understanding friend, my throat often hoarse with emotion, as I told her of my fights and frustration with the school system or the parties Max didn't get invited to or any of our other daily disasters ... Most friends would hear my tales of woe and express their empathy by jumping into the frenzy and stirring up my agitation. But that wasn't Patti. She would listen quietly...and when I was finished, she would say only one thing: 'They don't see the gift, Emily. They don't know Max is a gift.'[7]

It's often struck me, since reading this book, to question what kind of reaction I give people when they're upset about something. Do I 'stir up agitation' by agreeing that they've been grieved, by encouraging them to indulge the sense of

---

7.   Ibid, pp. 71-75.

hurt? Patti gives a wonderful example of pointing pain back to the Saviour. Through the pain, God is good.

In the way she reacts to Emily here, Patti lovingly makes two inferences: that the people who are upsetting Emily lack Emily's spiritual understanding; and that she should not lower her gaze to their level. Instead, she needs to keep her eyes fixed on Jesus. She needs to remain thankful. God is good even when other people are discouraging.

Patti did listen. She did acknowledge Emily's pain. She didn't judge her for feeling hurt or frustrated by difficult circumstances. But instead of adding to the frustration, she gave the true comfort of grounding Emily in who she was, who Max was, and who Jesus was.

Instead of adding to the frustration, she gave the true comfort of grounding Emily in who she was, who Max was, and who Jesus was.

One of Patti's striking characteristics in the book is that she is totally unfazed by Max's condition, even at his most uncontrollable. You would think this might be because of her background in special needs care, but in reality, Patti seemed to be unfazed by any trials that came her way. Perhaps I should say unshaken. She had the deep emotions everyone experiences, but nothing that life threw at her could take her eyes off Jesus at all. This single-mindedness is what she was able to pass on to all those around her. Even the prospect of dying from cancer, leaving a young family behind, Patti accepted as part of God's good plan. Her priority was not raging at the unfairness of her fate, or questioning why this would happen to her. It was preparing her own friends for her passing, and making sure she witnessed to everyone she came into contact with at the hospital! Of all the many, many people that mattered to Patti, Jesus mattered the most. And that was to the benefit of everyone around her.

> *Of all the many, many people that mattered to Patti, Jesus mattered the most. And that was to the benefit of everyone around her.*

What if you are a Mother Disappointed by the Church?

It's probably the lowest common denominator of citation to quote a meme, but seeing as the Lord uses even the humblest of circumstances to feed us, I'm going to pass on an uncredited thought that appears every so often on my Facebook feed. 'Many people turn from Jesus because of a bad experience with religious people. We must remember that Jesus also had a bad experience with religious people: He was crucified by them.'

We can see quite clearly in Scripture what the Church *should* look like. We should be tender toward one another, anticipating each other's needs, sacrificing to meet them, and forgiving easily. We have all had experiences where 'church people' have treated us far differently to this. Women of all stripes – whether single, wives, mothers, widows, or any other subset you can think of – have felt isolated, unseen, judged, treated unkindly or thoughtlessly, or overburdened. In church, we will find those who do not truly love or follow the Lord, and also those who simply follow Him imperfectly. There is not a single person, Christian or otherwise, that will not at some point disappoint us, given enough time. And there is not a single person that we will not disappoint, given enough time. You really understand the importance of forgiveness when you're the one in need of it!

You really understand the importance of forgiveness when you're the one in need of it!

If you've been hurt by the Church, fix your eyes on the Lord. He knows what that feels like. Those who should have been first to welcome and serve Him were those who tried to hamper His ministry and end His life. How did He react to those people? He did not excuse their behaviour, but He did hold out forgiveness for any who would take it.

One mother who knew those feelings more than most was Hagar. When Sarai and Abram couldn't conceive a child on their own, Sarai forced Hagar to sleep with Abram in order to conceive an heir. Now, Hagar wasn't perfect either – the Bible says that after she conceived, she 'despised' her mistress, or treated her with contempt. But after Abram washed his hands of all responsibility for the women's argument, Sarai treated her servant so cruelly that Hagar ran away.

Note that these were the people of God. Abram was 'the friend of God', and the father of a nation. Sarai ends up in the Hall of Faith in Hebrews. Yet they were acting out of fear that their worldly legacy would not be established, and that fear led them to treat with harshness someone whom they should have protected. People who genuinely love God can do terrible things. Sarai and Abram had already met with God and heard His promises, but they had not yet come into a deeper communion with Him

People who genuinely love God can do terrible things.

that would change their very identities as Sarah and Abraham. They were still a work in progress. So how do we see God's goodness to Hagar?

Hagar runs away to the wilderness, and there the Angel of the Lord – a personage often taken on by the Son of God before He was born as Jesus – finds her. And along with assuring her that He has a plan both for her and for the son she will bear, and that He has heard everything she's been through, He tells her what she probably least wants to hear: that she must go back and submit to her master and mistress.

The people of God are not yet perfect. But we still have a place and a purpose among them. We are not perfect. We need to be there among the growth and the grace and the forgiveness. That does not mean that we need to go back to a particular fellowship or relationship where we have been abused – the Lord does not lead us all on Hagar's personal path – but it does show that being

The people of God are not yet perfect. But we still have a place and a purpose among them.

let down by the Church is not an excuse for giving up on it. Because Jesus didn't. And because, as with Hagar, there is a provision He gives us when we feel we simply can't do it.

Look at Genesis 16:13 (NIV). She gave this name to the Lord who spoke to her: *'You are the God who sees me,' for she said, 'I have now seen the One who sees me.'*

El Roi: the God Who Sees.

If you have been hurt, if it feels impossible to walk back into that hurt or to forgive or to trust again, rest in the knowledge that our Jesus saw an abused and enslaved pregnant woman who had no hope. He sees what you've been through, He sees you in every painful and lonely moment, and He even sees your future and the plans He has for you. He is able to bring good out of it all. As He told Hagar: 'I will increase your descendants so much that they will be too numerous to count' (Gen. 16:10).

El Roi, who sees you, is also El Shaddai, Almighty God who can do all things.

How did Jesus Care for us?

The tenderness of the Lord isn't just shown in His care of women, or even just in His incarnation as Jesus. One of my favourite pictures of His sweet care is in 1 Kings 19. The prophet Elijah has just had a showdown with the prophets of Baal and God has demonstrated His power through Him. Rather than taking strength from that victory, though, Elijah is completely drained and runs away from King Ahab in fear of his life:

> *But he himself went a day's journey into the wilderness and came and sat down under a broom tree. And he asked that he might die, saying, 'It is enough; now, O Lord, take away my life, for I am no better than my fathers.' And he lay down and*

slept under a broom tree. And behold, an angel touched him and said to him, 'Arise and eat.' And he looked, and behold, there was at his head a cake baked on hot stones and a jar of water. And he ate and drank and lay down again. And the angel of the Lord came again a second time and touched him and said, 'Arise and eat, for the journey is too great for you.' And he arose and ate and drank, and went in the strength of that food forty days and forty nights to Horeb, the mount of God (1 Kings 19:4-8).

Have you ever felt so alone and so exhausted you just wanted it all to be over? These moments can hit us even on the way down from a spiritual high. Yet the Lord sees us with such great compassion and kindness. I love how He woke Elijah like a little child and ministered to Him. Sometimes we find it hard to accept the Lord serving us; we feel as if we must be constantly striving for Him. Yet we receive so much more from Him than we give!

Next time you feel completely worn out by life and unable to go on a day longer in your own strength, ask the Lord for His food that gives supernatural strength and renewal, and the loveliness of His own presence with it.

Verses about Caring for Mothers

Then children were brought to him that he might lay his hands on them and pray. The disciples rebuked the people, but Jesus said, 'Let the little children come to me and do not hinder them, for to such belongs the kingdom of heaven.' And he laid his hands on them and went away (Matt. 19:13-15).

The sweetness of this is that Jesus loves the helpless ones that we love. He is willing to touch them, bring them near, see them and value them. For single parents or those without much of a support network, it is literally thrilling to see someone else take a real interest or joy in the child who is dear to you. Jesus adores these little ones. If you can come alongside a mother and show love to her child, it just makes her heart sing in addition to whatever practical relief you are giving.

> *He will tend his flock like a shepherd; he will gather the lambs in his arms; he will carry them in his bosom, and gently lead those that are with young* (Isa. 40:11).

This passage reminds me of Psalm 23, showing in greater detail just how tender the coming Messiah would be with the sheep that 'knew His voice'. When you are caring for the young, you walk slowly. You walk in faith. You go at the young child's, or young Christian's, pace. You don't drive yourself to get to every blade of grass in the field all at once because they look untidy. You don't expect to travel as far or as fast as you did on your own. And in return, the shepherd guides you to the places where you can graze easily, where there is plenty. Where you are kept warm and secure by the rest of the flock. You are under His constant eye because – when you are with young – you are doing what He is doing. You are caring for and nurturing one of His lambs. He will guide and lead you gently in this work as you look to Him.

When you are with young – you are doing what He is doing. You are caring for and nurturing one of His lambs

Questions

1. Can you think of times during your life when you have been the dinner party guest, the exhausted mother, and Mrs Woods? How can your experiences of the latter two help you when you are tempted to look the other way from someone who is struggling?

2. Is there someone you can help practically – with a meal, grocery card, conversation, babysitting? Is there someone with whom you need to follow up on prayer requests? Remember what we discussed in the last chapter: you can serve even when your need is greater.

3. Have you thought of giving up on Church or on Christian people you know who have hurt you? How does it help to know El Roi, the God who sees, has compassionately seen all your hurt? Can you love His people for the sake of loving Him?

Song
Why should I feel discouraged,
Why should the shadows come?
Why should my heart be lonely,
And long for heaven and home
When Jesus is my portion,
My constant Friend is He;
His eye is on the sparrow,
And I know He watches over me.
'His Eye is On the Sparrow', Civilla D. Martin

8. A Godly Stepmother

Katherine Parr

Katherine Parr was the last of Henry VIII's six wives. She was an unusual choice for Henry: while his other wives had been chosen with a view to their youth, fertility and connections, Katherine was a more practical choice. She had already been widowed twice without producing any children; she brought no great political alliances. She did, however, hold the intelligence and moral fortitude that (while much maligned) had characterised both Catherine of Aragon and Anne Boleyn, the first two wives. It's possible that, having been often ruled by passion, and experienced failure to some degree in all five previous marriages, the king finally knew what he really needed. In his dying days, Katherine Parr provided him with compassion, stability, loyalty, wise counsel, and gospel love.

While she eased the end of Henry's life, Katherine's far greater influence was on his three children, Mary (daughter of Catherine of Aragon), Elizabeth (daughter of Anne Boleyn) and the heir, Edward (son of Jane Seymour). While her reign as queen was relatively brief and uneventful – in Tudor terms! – Katherine Parr has gone down as one of the great stepmothers of history. She made it one of the first acts of her marriage to request that the children have much greater access to their father, and to herself as well. She wrote to each of them individually, with kindness and affection, and with a focus on their spiritual wellbeing. Katherine appeared to approach the throne differently from each of her predecessors: not with an eye to her own future or career, but with a view to doing good to her new family, court and to the country.

The young Edward was drawn to his stepmother as a young boy, delighted with her interest in him, and there is no doubt she nurtured the motherless boy. Mary also enjoyed Katherine's company, though her Catholic beliefs, loyal to her own mother, remained a barrier between them. But it is the adolescent Elizabeth with whom Katherine had the real connection. They corresponded extensively when they could not be together, and at New Year, Elizabeth would present Katherine with personally translated and handwritten copies of Protestant writings. While Elizabeth's own claim to the throne depended on her upholding her mother's Protestant beliefs, she seemed also to have a personal interest in the things of the Lord that was much nurtured by her stepmother.

After her father's death, Elizabeth went to live with Katherine and her new husband, Thomas Seymour. There is some debate about what happened next. Seymour formed a habit of bursting into his new stepdaughter's bedchamber for tickle fights that she found both amusing and discomfiting; on another occasion, he cut her dress to shreds in the garden. Katherine seems to have found this entertaining – or acted as if she did; she took part in the early morning visits on occasion. It is difficult to tell whether she really interpreted it all as good fun, or she was being pressured by her husband (who displayed self-centred and amoral behaviour in general). When the finally pregnant Katherine found Elizabeth in Thomas' arms, she sent her away. Again, it is not known whether that was to protect Elizabeth or to protect her marriage. She continued to correspond with her stepdaughter until her death, a few months later, following childbirth.

In terms of her faith, Katherine Parr was not merely a political or superficial Protestant. Her beliefs were in the mould of Martin Luther, with his emphasis on salvation through grace alone. There were many dangers in her position: courtiers tried to threaten her life by telling Henry she was wearing the theological trousers in the family, necessitating Katherine to make a diplomatic apology for effectively showing too great intelligence in their discussions! And while Katherine was evangelical among her ladies-in-waiting and other household members, this too was fraught – one of her ladies, Anne Askew, was executed after refusing to refute her Reformed faith.

It is probably due much to her gentleness and diplomacy that Katherine was able to publish her theological works with impunity, and in fact wrote very popular devotionals. The best-known and most evangelical of these is *The Lamentation of a Sinner*. It is almost extravagant in its humility, certainly unheard of from a member of the Tudor royal family. It also presents Christ as the worthy, glorious and living Son of God, and calls out various factions of Tudor nobility and clergy for their hypocrisy and their need of repentance. It must have been electrifying to read this from the Queen's hand, whether a noble or a commoner, and certainly as a priest. With this work, Katherine was one of the earliest and most influential English voices for biblical Christianity, and it set her as a mother to the nation as well as to Henry's three children.

I professed Christ in my baptism, when I began to live (spiritually), but I swerved from him after baptism ... even as the heathen which never had begun. Christ was innocent and void of all sin, and I wallowed in filthy sin and was free from no sin. Christ was obedient unto his Father even to the death of the cross, and I disobedient, and most stubborn, even to the confusion of truth.

Christ was meek and humble in heart, and I most proud and vainglorious. Christ despised the world, with all the vanities thereof, and I made it my god because of the vanities. Christ came to serve his brethren, and I coveted to rule over them. Christ despised worldly honour, and I much delighted to attain the same. Christ loved the base and simple things of the world, and I esteemed the most fair and pleasant things. Christ loved poverty, and I wealth. Christ was gentle and merciful to the poor, and I hard-hearted and ungentle. Christ prayed for his enemies, and I hated mine. Christ rejoiced in the conversion of sinners, and I was not grieved to see their reversion to sin.

By this declaration, anyone may perceive how far I was from Christ and without Christ; yea, how contrary to Christ, although I bore the name of a Christian. Insomuch that if any man had said I had been without Christ, I would have stiffly withstood the same. And yet I neither knew Christ nor wherefore he came. As concerning the effect and purpose of his coming, I had a certain vain, blind knowledge, both cold and dead, which may be had with all sin: as it plainly appears by this my confession and open declaration.

Yet I never truly grasped the abundant love of God ... 'til it pleased God of his mere grace, mercy and pity to open mine eyes, making me to see...Christ crucified to be mine only saviour and redeemer. For then I began (and not before) to ... see mine own ignorance and blindness ... all pleasures, vanities, honour, riches, wealth and aids of the world began to taste bitter unto me. Then I knew it was no illusion of the devil, nor false nor human doctrine I had received, when this change came over me: that I was horrified by all the things I had before so much loved and esteemed, since God forbids that we should love the world or the vain pleasures and shadows in the same. Then began I to understand that Christ was my only saviour and redeemer, and the understanding of his holiness can only be given by grace unto faith, not by any human reason or wit. Then began I to dwell in God by love.

... I don't doubt that many will wonder and marvel at this, my saying that I never knew Christ for my saviour and redeemer, until this time; for many have this opinion, saying 'Who doesn't know about Christ? Everyone who calls themselves a Christian knows who He is.' And thus, believing their dead, human, historical faith and knowledge (which they have learned in their academic books) to be the true infused faith and knowledge of Christ ...

Neither life, honour, riches ... be it never so dearly beloved of me: but most willingly and gladly I would leave it to win any man to Christ whether or rich or poor. And yet is this nothing in comparison to the love that God showed in sending Christ to die for me ...

God knows how sincerely I have lamented mine own sins and faults to the world. I trust nobody will judge I have done it for praise or thank of any creature, since these are things which bring me shame and not joy. For if they know how little I esteem and weigh the praise of the world, they would have to change their opinion: for I thank God (by his grace), I know the world to be a blind judge, and their praise means nothing.[1]

* * *

Whoever receives one such child in my name receives me (Matt. 18:5).

One of the most interesting little-known stories of the Old Testament is a tale of two stepmothers. After her husband King Jehoram died, Queen Athaliah ordered the slaughter of all the royal princes so that she could rule in her own right. Jehoram's grown-up daughter, Jehosheba, was married to the high priest (this was perhaps not as influential as it sounds, given that Jehoram and his queen were essentially idol-worshippers and hostile to Temple worship). Jehosheba knew she could not save all of her brothers and half-brothers, but she could at least do something. She went to the palace, found the youngest of the babies, Prince Joash, and sneaked him and his nurse out. For seven years, Jehosheba and her husband hid Joash in the Temple, raising him alongside their own son. It's like something from a fairy tale – the boy's sister rescued him from an evil stepmother and then became a mother to him herself.[2]

1.　Full text available at https://newwhitchurch.press/parr/lamentation. I have modernized the text for easier reading.

2.　2 Chronicles 22-23.

It's clear that all the trauma of Joash's early life was part of God's plan. Rather than being raised in a pagan palace, he grew up in the Temple of the true God, and in an atmosphere of love and worship instead of decadence and intrigue. When he was crowned aged seven, Joash had his 'foster father', the High Priest Jehoiada, to help him rule. Joash was a godly king for most of his life and repaired the Lord's Temple.

The children of Henry VIII were in a similar position. Due to their father's veering between different theologies and politics in an attempt to secure his own legacy, both of his daughters' positions – and lives – were in constant danger, and they had virtually no personal relationship with him at all. Their favour with him was entirely predicated on his own ambition. This was the family that Katherine Parr was entering. What made her such a successful mother to his children, and how can we emulate her character whenever we stand *in loco parentis* to a child or vulnerable person?

Spiritual Self-care

Both Sarah Edwards and Amy Carmichael emphasized the importance of finding time to spend alone before the Lord. In times of busyness, it can feel impossible to carve out that time. Yet neglecting it leaves us open to so many attacks from the devil, specifically focused on that very motherhood: impatience, lack of compassion,

Impatience, lack of compassion, spiritual and mental exhaustion, all take hold when we are not taking the time to abide in the Lord.

spiritual and mental exhaustion, all take hold when we are not taking the time to abide in the Lord.

A member of the royal family may seem as though they would have all the time they need – look at all the servants and nannies! – but, in reality, the Queen would have been surrounded by people, and pressures, most of the time. Nevertheless, Katherine took time to read the Bible – judging by her understanding and quoting of Scripture, she knew it well – and to read the most important new theological works being published. This was dangerous in her day; the liberties of Protestantism were fragile, and true believers were still seen as subversive. Yet Katherine found time to read about the Lord, to consider His things deeply and humbly with an open mind, and to write about her own conversion experience in a way that did not focus upon herself but upon Jesus and His beauty.

Compassion for the Past

When Katherine entered Henry's family, she saw it as just that – a family. Not a step up for her, not a political manoeuvre. She saw the children not as political players but as children. And she had compassion on what they had already been through with their mercurial father and tragic mothers. It would have been easy for Katherine to decide not to rock the boat – that Henry's dealings with his children were his own responsibility and she need not interfere. Instead, she saw the children suffering by their removal from family, and she took responsibility beyond what was required. She saw that this family could be better than it was, and that the children could learn to love each other, and love their father, instead of being pitted against each other. She reached out to them in friendship and, while she wrote to them of Christ from the very first, she backed up this witness by providing the help and care they needed.

She saw the children suffering by their removal from family, and she took responsibility beyond what was required.

The book of James reminds us that 'faith without works is dead'. This doesn't mean that we are saved by good works, but it asks the question, 'What does salvation look like?' Our goodness, patience, generosity and so on toward others is the proof of what the Lord is doing in our own hearts. In Chapter 2, verse 16, James says, '*If a brother or sister is poorly clothed and lacking in daily food, and one of you says to them, "Go in peace, be warmed and filled," without giving them the things needed for the body, what good is that?*' Katherine did not take the easy road of simply wishing her stepchildren well. She wrote openly of the faith inside her heart and then demonstrated it practically.

How tempting it is to see people in terrible positions in society and start to blame or look down on them instead of nurturing compassion for the dark path they've travelled. If we can blame them, of course, we need not (in fact, we cannot) take responsibility ourselves for helping them. If we can see people as undeserving, we can justify ourselves withholding any good we could do them. In fact, when we see people as undeserving, this should remind us to show grace. What is grace but offering favour to those who don't deserve it? We should show grace to everyone because we have received grace – far more than we could ever give to someone else.

Godly Character with an Ungodly Partner

Katherine began her married life as a peacemaker between the three very different children and their father. She saw that a closer family unit would do them all good, and she made it her mission to bring about that good in the sphere she had been given. Bear in mind that Katherine never wanted to marry Henry. When she received his proposal, she was already planning to marry Thomas Seymour. She had no desire to be queen and certainly no romantic inclinations toward the ageing and unstable king. So when she married him, her decision may have been forced by the consequences of turning him down – but her behaviour within the marriage was motivated by a desire to bring peace and Christian love to the royal household.

Katherine lived her life with upstanding Christian conscientiousness even though her husband professed faith without any evidence of true belief. She did not lecture him about his behaviour or his theology, but gently led him into discussion when she could. When Henry's courtiers wanted to get rid of Katherine, they accused her of presumptuously trying to teach him theology. Katherine learned of this and went straight to Henry with an apology, stating that she had not meant to preach to him. She overcame his notorious temper with gentleness and humility. A soft answer turned away wrath, and in fact he was then indignant with the men who had tried to come between them.

Whether married or not, we often partner with others in ministry or in the nurturing of others – whether teachers who work on a staff, working in Sunday School under a minister's direction, fostering in partnership with a social worker, or carrying out missionary work through an organisation. We rarely minister in an isolated bubble. And getting on with others is always a challenge. There are times when direct confrontation is needed (our colleagues and spouses are not, after all, a king!). Yet we can do so much good when we simply treat all of those around us, whether colleagues or family members or children, as gently and patiently as Christ treats us.

Katherine not only ministered to Henry as a wife; she also encouraged him to take part in his children's lives and to think well of them. Even if this would have disadvantaged any children she herself had while consort, she valued the broken relationships around her and actively worked toward their healing.

One Eye on the Future

Katherine Parr was acutely aware of the potential of Henry's children. While Edward was the heir apparent at that time, he was never strong, and Katherine knew that each of the children would have their role to play in the life of the nation, whether that was making important marriages and alliances or sitting on the throne themselves. Each child had the potential to change the world around them, and to change their country. They would not be locked away and isolated from court life forever – and God could use them.

Do we see the children and vulnerable people around us as those who are valuable in God's kingdom? Or do we see them as limited, irrelevant or

I am convicted to think how seldom I think of those around me as vessels of God's unlimited power!

burdensome? I am convicted to think how seldom I think of those around me as vessels of God's unlimited power! Our children may not grow up to sit on a throne, but they can serve One who does, and through Him they too have the power to change the world.

Paul told Timothy to '*let no one despise your youth*'.[3] But often, I despise my children's youth. How humbled I am when I hear them, in their still lisping voices, suddenly come out with some truth about God, a profession of love for Jesus, or a prayer I didn't know they were capable of praying. Let us ask the Lord to raise up our children, and the children whose lives are precious to us, as those who will change the world for Him. May we set them apart as Samuel was set apart to the Lord from birth, with the purpose of bringing them continually into God's presence. Let us teach them seriously and lovingly of Him from the very start, as Katherine did with her stepchildren.

> *Paul told Timothy to* 'let no one despise your youth'. *But often, I despise my children's youth.*

Education, Education, Education

One of the practical interests that Katherine took in the children's lives was that of their education. She encouraged them not only to excel in their studies but to enjoy them. She did this primarily by taking an interest in what they did, which motivated them to do well and to please her. Kids may do well

---

3.   1 Timothy 4:12 (NKJV).

at school when they are simply interested in their subjects or want to reach their own goals; but when they want to please someone who loves them, they simply shine.

Elizabeth gives a poignant example of this: for New Year, she presented her stepmother with a personally translated and handwritten translation of Marguerite of Navarre's *Mirror or Glass of the Sinful Soul* (her copy is now in the Bodleian library). She was eleven years old! The following year she made a similar project of some of John Calvin's works. Katherine poured into Elizabeth's life, and Elizabeth rewarded her with a loving, thoughtful and time-consuming gift which showed her gratitude.

Katherine did not only value her stepchildren's education, but also their gifts and talents. Elizabeth would have been a clever and gifted child (and ruler) without Katherine's input, but it was her stepmother who gave her a warmth and understanding that she carried with her. Because Katherine showed love, Elizabeth was also willing to take correction and hard truths from her. Even after she was compelled to leave her stepmother's household, Elizabeth wrote thanking Katherine for her ongoing willingness to tell the princess of any negative gossip she might hear about her.

When they Don't Make it Easy

The children of Henry VIII were primed to make model stepchildren, in a way – they had been starved of natural family affection, and conditioned (both through courtly society and through political intimidation) to show respect to those in authority over them. But however stepchildren come into our lives, they have usually been through great trials, whether the illness or incapacity or death or the divorce of their parents. And often, unlike Henry's children, the stepchildren of the twenty-first century still have a relationship with both biological parents, which can add complications and tension to building something new with an adoptive or stepmother. If adopted or stepchildren are uninterested or actively hostile to a new parent, the story may look very different.

We will look further down at what God looks like as an adoptive parent. But in this section it is helpful just to stop and think for a moment about what we looked like as His prospective children. We were, without exception, either indifferent or hostile to His offer of a new life under His authority and protection. We insulted Him, mocked Him, mistrusted Him, rebelled against Him, and refused the gratitude He was due. Yet through all this, He persisted in calling us into His family. What's more, we continue even after adoption to go our own way, to neglect Him, to try being self-sufficient, and to act embarrassed to be seen with Him! Yet He never stops pursuing us, loving us, forgiving us, and calling us back home.

We continue even after adoption to go our own way, to neglect Him, to try being self-sufficient, and to act embarrassed to be seen with Him! Yet He never stops pursuing us, loving us, forgiving us, and calling us back home.

We are being gradually ever more conformed to Christ, and it is not just for our own sakes. It is equipping us to show others the same grace we have been given. Children, in their natural selfishness, can try our patience and our love more than anyone else. It is only our abiding in Jesus that can prepare us to bear with them as He bears with us.

But the Increase is God's

The story of Joash does not have a happy ending. As long as his foster-parents were alive, Joash was an excellent ruler and maintained a consistent walk before the Lord. As soon as Jehoiada the High Priest died, however, his heart started to stray. It wasn't long before he was walking in rebellion from God, and even had his foster-brother, the priest Zechariah, murdered in the courtyard of the Temple.

Katherine Parr's three stepchildren did not always walk in godly ways either. Edward died young, but Mary, who maintained her Catholic faith despite Katherine's example, reigned briefly before going out in a flame of bloody vindictiveness against Protestants. Elizabeth, while in many ways a great ruler, also had her palace intrigues and treated some evangelicals cruelly.

We can't control the choices our children, and the dear ones we care for, will make when they are grown. Sometimes, they will turn away from God (even as we all have done at times) and 'a sword will pierce our own hearts', in quite a different way than was experienced by the mother of Jesus. Sometimes, they may grow up without accepting our faith. They may make

We can't control the choices our children, and the dear ones we care for, will make when they are grown.

disastrous choices. They may set themselves as enemies of the Lord that we love. And we will grieve, and we will pray, and we will continue to love the Lord and to love our children.

Paul says, 'I planted, Apollos watered, but God gave the growth.'[4] We can only do what we can do – we serve God faithfully by living out an example of loving and godly faith; we show compassion for past hurts and sins; we live at peace with our fellow-workers; we nurture our children's potential and giftings and pray for God to woo them and to use them. This is what we can do. Katherine Parr went above and beyond in caring, in all these ways, for those whom God had brought into her life. Through Elizabeth, she ministered to a nation. Who knows how far her influence went to temper the future queen's character and decisions? God can do wonderful things through our legacy of faith.

Jesus as Our Adoptive Father

[Jesus] entered Jericho and was passing through. And behold, there was a man named Zacchaeus. He was a chief tax collector and was rich. And he was seeking to see who Jesus was, but on account of the crowd he could not, because he was small in stature. So he ran on ahead and climbed up into a sycamore tree to see him, for he was about to pass that way. And when Jesus came to the place, he looked up and said to him, 'Zacchaeus, hurry and come down, for I must stay at your house today.' So he hurried and came down and received him joyfully. And when they saw it, they all grumbled, 'He has gone in to be the guest of a man who is a sinner.' And Zacchaeus stood and said

---

4.   1 Corinthians 3:6.

to the Lord, 'Behold, Lord, the half of my goods I give to the poor. And if I have defrauded anyone of anything, I restore it fourfold.' And Jesus said to him, 'Today salvation has come to this house, since he also is a son of Abraham. For the Son of Man came to seek and to save the lost' (Luke 19:1-10).

The story of Zacchaeus may seem like an odd one to illustrate adoption. But look at the before and after story of Zacchaeus. Here was a man who was hated, an outcast, and that because of the wrong he himself had done in colluding with the Romans to cheat his own people. He was rich but so desperate for peace that he was willing, ridiculously, to climb a tree just to get a glimpse of whether Jesus might be able to provide an answer. He probably had a great house, but it couldn't have been much of a home when no respectable person would set foot inside it.

Jesus makes it a home. He takes Zacchaeus' humility and loneliness and converts them to honour and fellowship. Without even having to be told to make amends, this taste that Jesus gives him of restoration makes Zacchaeus want to repent and make restitution. And, through Jesus' one act of kindness and the repentance that follows, Zacchaeus is set in a family: 'He also is a son of Abraham.' He is in Christ's family, the Jewish family, the community family. An unwanted, defiant and desperate person now has love, guidance and belonging. If that isn't adoption, what is?

Verses on Adoption

Our journey toward God as our Father starts 'while we were still sinners',[5] when Jesus comes to meet us in the hopelessness and corruption of life without Him. He reaches down to pull us 'out of the miry bog',[6] to set us on the solid ground of His love and truth. Even though we owe God everything, He does not make us mere servants in His household, but beloved children with full access to His presence and an inheritance with His begotten Son, Jesus.[7] Even though Jesus paid a great price for our adoption, He is fully satisfied with us as His reward, and presents us to the Father with overwhelming joy.[8]

God promises, along with our salvation through Jesus' sacrifice, to 'graciously give us all things'[9] that we need to live as members of His family. And not only do we have a Father, but we have also been integrated into a unit with new brothers and sisters, mothers and fathers.[10] Our inheritance is not only to remain part of God's kingdom, but actually to reign through eternity as part of His royal family![11]

Along with inheritance and belonging, God also gives us a home. He has promised to prepare this for us when it comes time for us to go and live with Him;[12] and His home means

---

5.   Romans 5:8.

6.   Psalm 40:2.

7.   Romans 8:17.

8.   Jude 1:24.

9.   Romans 8:32.

10.   Matthew 19:29.

11.   2 Timothy 2:11-13.

12.   John 14:3.

not only an actual house, but security and rest and joy in His physical presence.[13]

The totality of our acceptance by our Heavenly Father can only be encapsulated in Jesus' own words in John 15:9 – some of His last words to His friends before going to His death, in fact. 'As the Father has loved me, so have I loved you. Abide in my love.'

Questions

1. What people do you know who have been rejected or are apart from their own family? God promises to 'set the orphans in a family' – how can you be part of His work in this respect?
2. Consider the young or vulnerable people you know, and the limitless potential they have in God's Kingdom. How can you more effectively pray for them, example them, and encourage them to be world-changers for Christ?
3. Consider what it means to be adopted by God. What characteristics do you see in Him as a Father? How can you reflect these in family resemblance as His child?

Song

Beneath the cross of Jesus
His family is my own
Once strangers chasing selfish dreams,
Now one through grace alone.
How could I now dishonour

---

13. 1 John 3:2.

The ones that You have loved?
Beneath the cross of Jesus
See the children called by God.
–'Beneath the cross of Jesus', Kristyn Getty

9. A Mother who Suffered

Elizabeth Prentiss

Elizabeth Prentiss grew up in the north of the United States and, as a mature woman, observed with horror the American Civil War. She was the wife of the minister George Prentiss and bore many children, two of whom died in infancy or toddlerhood. She was also a frequent sufferer of often debilitating illness characterised by headaches, insomnia and depression. For all that, Elizabeth was a lively, loving and grateful person; reading her letters, collected and annotated by her husband after death, gives one the feeling of conversing with Jo March from *Little Women*! Elizabeth was a prolific Christian writer in her time and is best remembered for the novel *Stepping Heavenward*.

Despite her cheerful nature, there were times when she expressed deep anguish and almost an inability to function. In this chapter, we'll discuss several types of suffering that Elizabeth underwent, as well as the lessons she would pass on to us.

* * *

When the cares of my heart are many, your consolations cheer my soul (Ps. 94:19).

Ordinary Suffering

You don't have to be bereaved or chronically ill to suffer in motherhood. There is no exhaustion like that of baby-induced sleep deprivation, or worse, young-adult-induced sleep deprivation! The mental weariness of hearing the same questions and demands all day, with little adult conversation to dilute it and little time for my own interests, has been at times a tremendous struggle that has left me feeling downright haggard. Given her sunny disposition, it cheered me to no end to see that Elizabeth Prentiss sometimes felt the same way! Here she describes episodes with her babies and young children:

> I find the care of [the baby] very wearing, and have cried ever so many times from fatigue and anxiety, but now I am getting a little better and she pays me for all I do.[1]

> By far the greatest trial I have to contend with, is that of losing all power to control my time. A little room all of my own, and a regular hour, morning and night, all of my own would enable me, I think, to say, 'Now let life do its worst!'[2]

> [When I am in] pain, dizzy, faint and exhausted with suffering, starvation, and sleeplessness, it is terrible to have to walk the room with a crying child! I thought as I lay, worn out even to childishness, obliged for the baby's sake to have a bright sunlight streaming into the chamber, and to keep my eyes and ears on the alert for the same cause, how still we used to think the house must be left when my father had

---

1. *The Life and Letters of Elizabeth Prentiss* by George L. Prentiss - Full Text Free Book (Part 5/13) (fulltextarchive.com), p. 338.
2. Ibid, p. 369.

these headaches and how mother busied herself all day long about him, and how nice his little plate of hot steak used to look, as he sat up to eat it when the sickness had gone – and how I am suffering here all alone with nobody to give me even a look of encouragement. George was out of town on my sickest day. When he was at home he did everything in the world he could do to keep the children still, but here they must be and I must direct about every trifle and have them on the bed with me. I am getting desperate and feel disposed to run furiously in the traces till I drop dead on the way. Don't think me very wicked for saying so. I am jaded in soul and body and hardly know what I do want.[3]

One of the sermons that has stuck with me over the years from my minister, Derek Lamont, is one where he showed us that sometimes what we take for spiritual weakness is actually no more than physical weakness. When we feel overburdened and laden with anxiety and guilt, what is actually happening sometimes is not an experience of God's displeasure with something in our lives, but a simple mental strain or depression or exhaustion. I have had those times when, feeling an inability to 'connect' spiritually, I wore myself out praying and

Sometimes what we take for spiritual weakness is actually no more than physical weakness.

worrying about some relatively small thing I'd done and could not feel peace or forgiveness for. It is difficult to see in the moment, but that is probably the time to seek rest and comfort in the Lord. To remember His tenderness, His delight in us. If

---

3.   Ibid, p. 373.

you are an overthinker, like me, it's easy to let your mind run on the negative – on the anxieties and shortcomings we all experience. Instead, our minds should be running to Christ for renewal. By all means let confession and repentance do its work: and then leave it there, and ask Him for rest. True spiritual rest is not something we get by traipsing over mountains and gorges in a mad search. It's something that we cannot obtain for ourselves and must be given to us, by faith.

The longer I walk through motherhood, the more I see that I am just like my children. I don't feel wise or independent or mature. I still have angry tantrums and inexplicable mood swings and spill things and feel small when someone is upset with me. I still feel helpless and afraid of the unknown and easily overwhelmed. I'm going to go back again to my favourite verse of the last year, Isaiah 46:4, '*Even to your old age I am he, and to grey hairs I will carry you. I have made, and I will bear; I will carry and will save.*' I am so glad my God is patient and tender toward me. And He is the same no matter how weary I am, and how dimly I can see Him. Elizabeth, of course, reached her own conclusion about our suffering:

> *I am just like my children. I don't feel wise or independent or mature. I still have angry tantrums and inexplicable mood swings and spill things and feel small when someone is upset with me. I still feel helpless and afraid of the unknown and easily overwhelmed.*

It is hard now to suffer, but after all, the light affliction is nothing, and the weight of glory is everything. You may not fully realise this or any other truth, in your enfeebled state, but truth remains the same whether we appreciate it or not; and so does Christ. Your despondency does not prove that HE is not just as near to you as He is to those who see Him more clearly; and it is better to be despondent than to be self-righteous. Don't you see that in afflicting you He means to prove to you that He loves you, and that you love Him? Don't you remember that it is His son – not His enemy – that He [disciplines]?[4]

The Suffering of Sickness

Elizabeth's description of looking after her children when feeling sick as a dog herself almost makes me smile! Mothers get help, but you rarely get a real 'sick day' with small kids. It's the same for true spiritual mothers too: when you're needed, you're needed, no matter what's going on in your own life.

> I know all about those depressed moods, when it costs one as much to smile, or to give a pleasant answer, as it would at other times to make a world. What a change it will be to us poor sickly, feeble, discouraged ones, when we find ourselves where there is neither pain or lassitude or fatigue of the body, or sorrow or care or despondency of the mind![5]

How often do I give 'a pleasant answer' or a smile when I am wakened in the night to tend to a child? We waste a lot of time and energy in resisting, or for that matter resenting, what we have to do anyway. What a blessing we would receive in knowing we had done these things instead with a willing and thankful heart. Attitudes are something we can't change

---

4.   Ibid, p. 802.
5.   Ibid, p. 404.

by ourselves. We are, so to speak, addicts to anger, irritation, comfort and personal space. We need Jesus to change us. We need Him to root out all of these things in our hearts, through constant deep repentance, and not only that but to replace them with His selflessness, compassion,

We are, so to speak, addicts to anger, irritation, comfort and personal space. We need Jesus to change us.

and readiness to love. Again, don't try to accomplish this in your own strength. Ask Him for His.

Paul Tripp's book on parenting, *Age of Opportunity*, drew my attention to the idolatry I had imposed on me-time and me-space. These are reasonable desires, but should never become so disproportionate that we justify ourselves overreacting to our children, or other loved ones, for placing quite normal demands on us. Paul speaks about various parenting idols we may entertain, and the section that struck me is this:

> Secretly in our hearts, many of us want life to be a resort. A resort is a place where you are the one who is served. Your needs come first, and you only do what you want to do when you want to do it. The only demands you deal with in a resort are the demands you put on yourself. At a resort, you live with a sense of entitlement. You've paid your money, and you have the right to expect certain things. I am afraid that many of us live for comfort and bring this entitlement mentality to our parenting. We reason that we have the right to quiet, harmony, peace, and respect, and we respond in anger when we do not get it.[6]

6. Page 31. Chapter 2 of *Age of Opportunity* can be accessed free online: https://assets.speakcdn.com/assets/1804/excerpt_age_of_opportunity.pdf

Contrast that selfish attitude, and the strife it brings, with this verse: '*Do not be conformed to this world, but be transformed by the renewal of your mind, that by testing you may discern what is the will of God, what is good and acceptable and perfect.*'[7] I love it because it gives hope. We don't have to say 'this is just how I feel and I can't help it' – no, we don't have to be enslaved to oppressive feelings like these. The Lord can transform us by the renewing of our mind! Then we will be able to focus on His will, what is good and acceptable and perfect. But we must be willing to be transformed. My favourite lesson from Elizabeth is this: '... I think [these misgivings] the result of the wish without the will to be holy. We pray for sanctification and then are afraid God will sanctify us by stripping us of our idols and feel distressed lest we cannot have them and Him too.'[8] How often my personal space or comfort has been my idol, especially when I'm unwell or anxious about something and feeling sorry for myself! Yet, even in those moments, I still have the work that God has called me to, and I am still called to be thankful in the midst of it.

The Suffering of Child Loss

In the early 1850s, George and Elizabeth lost a toddler son and an infant daughter. Elizabeth, soon after the first loss, wrote to a friend:

> We miss him sadly. I need not explain to you, who know all about it, how sadly; but we rejoice that he has got away from this troublous life, and that we have had the privilege of giving so dear a child to God ... God has been most merciful

---

7.   Romans 12:2.

8.   Prentiss, p. 369.

to us in this affliction, and, if a bereaved, we are still a happy household and full of thanksgiving.[9]

This upright attitude to suffering can seem over-holy to us, even unfeeling. Bereavement in the Bible is always greeted with sorrow, even if tempered by hope of reunion. Sometimes, I have found a Puritan attitude of giving thanks through grief off-putting. But, when you look deeper, you see a mother glorifying God to a friend while still taking her grief to Him in private. Note George's description of his bereft wife:

> But although the death of these two children tore with anguish the mother's heart, she made no show of grief, and to the eye of the world her life soon appeared to move on as aforetime. Never again, however, was it exactly the same life. She had entered into the fellowship of Christ's sufferings, and the new experience wrought a great change in her whole being ... But a cloud rested still upon her home, and at times the old grief came back again with renewed poignancy. Here are a few lines expressive of her feelings.
>
> They were written in pencil on a little scrap of paper:

My Nursery. 1852.
I thought that prattling boys and girls
Would fill this empty room;
That my rich heart would gather flowers
From childhood's opening bloom.
One child and two green graves are mine,
This is God's gift to me;
A bleeding, fainting, broken heart –
This is my gift to Thee.[10]

---

9.   Ibid, p. 432.
10. Ibid, pp. 446-447.

There is certainly a place for sharing our griefs and troubles with friends, especially in the Church, but I wonder if we remember to turn our deepest, wordless pain primarily to the Lord who sees all. We can go to Him groaning, or numb, yet in a spirit of submission, rather than of spirit of complaint or accusation. The consolation does not always come at once. But we are never unheard, and it does come.

Feb. 3rd – [During a child's near-fatal illness] The stupor, or whatever it is, in which that dreadful night has left me, is on me still. I have no more sense or feeling than a stone. I kneel down before God and do not say a word. I take up a book and read, but get hold of nothing. At church I felt

We can go to Him groaning, or numb, yet in a spirit of submission, rather than of spirit of complaint or accusation.

afraid I should fall upon the people and tear them. I could wish no one to pity me or even know that I am smitten. It does seem to me that those who can sit down and cry, know nothing of misery.

Feb. 4th – At last the ice melts and I can get near my God – my only comfort, my only joy, my All in all! This morning I was able to open my heart to Him and to cast some of this burden on Him, who alone knows what it is ... I see that it is sweet to be a pilgrim and a stranger, and that it matters very little what befalls me on the way to my blessed home. If God pleases to spare my child a little longer, I will be very thankful. May He take this season, when earthly comfort fails me, to turn me more than ever to Himself. For some months I have enjoyed a great deal in Him. Prayer has been very sweet and I have had some glimpses of joys indescribable.[11]

11. Ibid, pp. 467-468.

You may have heard of the musical *Hamilton*, based on the life of the first US Secretary of the Treasury. One of the most moving parts of the show comes in the second half, when Alexander and Eliza Hamilton's eldest son, Philip, is killed. Narrating the scene, Eliza's sister sings:

> *There are moments that the words don't reach*
> *There is suffering too terrible to name*
> *You hold your child as tight as you can*
> *And push away the unimaginable.*
> *The moments when you're in so deep*
> *It feels easier to just swim down ...*
> *We push away what we can never understand,*
> *We push away the unimaginable.* [12]

Losing the ones we love the most is probably one of our greatest fears. It feels literally unimaginable, even unsurvivable. Yet, even with the greatest losses can come a new knowledge, submission and reliance on the Lord – and even new blessing.

I've heard it said that, though we use the word 'widow' for a woman who has lost her husband, there is no word for a woman who has lost her child. She remains still, simply, a mother. I think there's a profound truth there, whether that is for a woman who has experienced miscarriage or infant loss, the death of a son or daughter in the faith – even those who have undergone abortion, which so often carries its own unique form of mourning.

Nor is death the only form of loss we undergo with our children. There may be the desertion – disappointment – betrayal of those we have loved. Those too can feel like deaths,

---

12. Lin-Manuel Miranda, *Hamilton,* 'It's Quiet Uptown.'

and I suppose we have all experienced them to some extent. It is so good to know that our Saviour also underwent every trial we go through in this respect! And it is a constant comfort that, when we have no words for our grief or our upheaval, '*the Spirit helps us in our weakness. For we do not know what to pray for as we ought, but the Spirit himself intercedes for us with groanings too deep for words. And he who searches hearts knows what is the mind of the Spirit, because the Spirit intercedes for the saints according to the will of God.*'[13]

Lessons from Suffering

Elizabeth, in her extensive correspondence, shared with her friends what she had learned through the paths on which God had led her. One which I found helpful was a retrospection on the uselessness of dwelling on our fears:

> They imagine that if such a dear friend were to die, or such and such blessings to be removed, they should be miserable; whereas God can make them a thousand times happier without them. To mention my own case: God has been depriving me of one blessing after another; but as every one was removed, He has come in and filled up its place; and now, when I am a cripple and not able to move, I am happier than ever I was in my life before or ever expected to be; and if I had believed this twenty years ago, I might have been spared much anxiety.[14]

We hold so tight to the things and the people we think we need. And we neglect to think of God, of faith, as something

---

13. Romans 8:26-27.
14. Prentiss, p. 309.

that brings happiness at all. We tend to think it brings privileges, or duties, or salvation, or peace, but not happiness. I often pray that I will find all of my delight increasingly in Jesus, not in other things. Elizabeth recognised that after the Lord healed one of her children, 'we ought to love Him better than we ever did. I do so want my weary solitude to bear that fruit.'[15] And I want my weariness and solitude to bear that fruit too: 'More love to Thee.'

We neglect to think of God, of faith, as something that brings happiness at all.

Aside from the spiritual insights she gleaned from suffering, Elizabeth received the ability to minister to others. She showed an eagerness to provide practical aid to others who had experienced chronic illness – and thus make her own sickness fruitful – and she became particularly suited to comfort those who were bereaved. George wrote, 'The sickness and death of little children wrought upon her with singular power; and, in ministering aid and comfort to bereaved mothers, she seemed like one specially anointed of the Lord for this gentle office.'[16]

> I literally love the house of mourning better than the house of feasting. All my long, long years of suffering and sorrow make sorrow-stricken homes homelike, and I can not but feel, because I know it from experience, that Christ loves to be in such homes. So you may congratulate me, dear, if I may be permitted to go where He goes.[17]

15. Ibid, p. 603.
16. Ibid, p. 318.
17. Ibid, p. 817.

Do you have the will – as well as the wish – to be holy? Then ask the Lord to make you more like Him, and to make Him your delight, and don't be afraid of how He will answer.

There may be suffering involved, but it will be used as a means of grace. To His people, He is always so much more merciful than He is

> *Christ loves to be in such homes. So you may congratulate me, dear, if I may be permitted to go where He goes.*

fearful. Pain will come whether we submit ourselves to Him or not. But if we do, then delight and fruitfulness comes with it, as surely as harvest after rain.

How do we see Jesus Suffering?
Ordinary suffering

> *And he answered them, 'O faithless generation, how long am I to be with you? How long am I to bear with you? Bring him to me'* (Mark 9:19).

When I feel this sensation of 'How long will I put up with this?!' it tends to be more exasperated than, as with Jesus' meaning, pained for someone else's sake! Yet it's comforting that He too felt the exhaustion of carrying on, bearing with people, when it was mentally and emotionally exhausting. *MacLaren's Expositions* brings out the meaning of Jesus' 'sigh' beautifully:

> The first thing that seems to be in the words is not anger, indeed, but a very distinct and very pathetic expression of Christ's infinite pain, because of man's faithlessness. The element of personal sorrow is most obvious here. It is not only

that He is sad for their sakes that they are so unreceptive, and He can do so little for them ... I shall have something to say about that presently ... but that He feels for Himself, just as we do in our poor humble measure, the chilling effect of an atmosphere where there is no sympathy.[18]

> *To His people, He is always so much more merciful than He is fearful.*

Suffering with need

> *Then Jesus was led up by the Spirit into the wilderness to be tempted by the devil. And after fasting forty days and forty nights, he was hungry. And the tempter came and said to him, 'If you are the Son of God, command these stones to become loaves of bread.' But he answered, 'It is written, "Man shall not live by bread alone, but by every word that comes from the mouth of God"' (Matt. 4:1-4).*

We don't see Jesus experience ill health, but we do see Him experience hunger and homelessness and exhaustion. I find it interesting that Satan attacks Jesus when He has communed with the Spirit during forty days of suffering. It might seem an obvious moment for temptation, at a point of physical weakness – but I suspect it was a moment of great spiritual strength, after forty days of uninterrupted communion and reliance on the Father. When Satan attacks us because of our outward weakness of tiredness or sickness or fasting, let's be sure that he finds us spiritually invincible because we have used these things as tools to draw nearer to the Lord.

---

18. https://biblehub.com/commentaries/mark/9-19.htm

Jesus suffering bereavement

*Soon afterward he went to a town called Nain, and his disciples
and a great crowd went with him. As he drew near to the gate
of the town, behold, a man who had died was being carried
out, the only son of his mother, and she was a widow, and a
considerable crowd from the town was with her. And when the
Lord saw her, he had compassion on her and said to her, 'Do
not weep.' Then he came up and touched the bier, and the
bearers stood still. And he said, 'Young man, I say to you, arise'*
(Luke 7:11-14).

Cosmo Panzetta – whose commentary on the 'woman of valour'
introduced this book – described a scene once of two crowds.[19]
One crowd, travelling with Jesus, is on an incredible high. They
have seen miracles. They have experienced healing. They have
been given words of dazzling life and indescribable hope. As they
follow Him toward a village, however, they meet another crowd:
a group of mourners accompanying a mother who is burying her
only son, wailing and beating their breasts and crying.

It sounds like a bit of a downer. Jesus might heal people
temporarily, but at the end of it – there is still death. A shadow
falls over the crowd, intruding on their joy. But what does
Jesus do? He raises the woman's son back to life!

You see, there is no end to His healing. There is no shadow
to His joy. There is no end, except the one He Himself will
experience on His people's behalf – and even that He will
defeat. Jesus is the Master over everything, even death. He

---

19.   https://www.youtube.com/watch?v=WRRs1KpxcNk, 10 July 2021, 'A Tale
of Two Crowds'.

used that woman's loss to glorify His Father. Even death is a tool that He uses to show His power and His love.

Interestingly enough, we never see in the Gospels a clear picture of Jesus encountering a death which He didn't defeat. We don't see Him react to His stepfather Joseph's passing, before His public ministry begins; we only see Him raising the dead. The only time we see Him submitting to death is in His own. And even then, He does not submit to death, but to His Father. 'Into your hands I commit my spirit.' Jesus felt the pain of death's parting so much it is as if He refused to countenance it. As the wonderful *Jesus Storybook Bible* puts it, 'He was making even death come untrue.'[20]

Verses on Suffering

... the Lord is at hand; do not be anxious about anything, but in everything by prayer and supplication with thanksgiving let your requests be made known to God. And the peace of God, which surpasses all understanding, will guard your hearts and your minds in Christ Jesus (Phil. 4:5-7).

Part of suffering is the anxiety which so often accompanies it. When you are having a hard time, you can often think things will only get worse; added to actual suffering is dread. In what way do we see the peace that passes all understanding?

---

20. Sally Lloyd-Jones, *The Jesus Storybook Bible: Anglicised Edition* (Grand Rapids: Zondervan, 2012), p 317. I can't recommend Sally Lloyd-Jones' storybook Bible enough, whether you have children or not. This quotation is from the chapter on Jesus' resurrection.

We don't see that peace from just laying our requests before the Lord once, and then turning back to worrying over our own fears and solutions. We have the peace while we are praying to Him, bringing Him our burdens, giving Him thanks, and focusing on the reality that 'He is at hand'. Note that that little phrase, for some reason chopped into verse 5, really belongs to verse 6. Why can we have such peace? Not because of our own prayers, but because the Lord is at hand. It's that focusing theme popping up again. When our attention is on Him, we have that peace that passes understanding. When our attention is on our problems, our anxieties loom again. Take them back to the Throne:

And after you have suffered a little while, the God of all grace, who has called you to his eternal glory in Christ, will himself restore, confirm, strengthen, and establish you (1 Pet. 5:10).

Remember that suffering always has a purpose. It's not for nothing. It's not arbitrary or cruel. You cannot fulfil God's ultimate purposes for you without ever suffering, and suffering well. Christ suffered; He calls us to be refined too. It doesn't feel like 'a little while' when you're going through it. But ask Him for just a glimpse of what He is doing – that restoration, confirmation, strengthening and establishing of your character – and you will be reassured by His drawing nearer, by the insights you gain into Bible passages that never struck you before, by seeing a growing Christlikeness in your reactions and attitudes and desires. Make it count.

Precious in the sight of the LORD is the death of his saints (Ps. 116:15).

Even though death is unnatural in the sense it was never in God's perfect design for our world, He delights to bring His loved ones home to His perfect heaven! For Him, their deaths are not a tragedy but a joy. As the martyr Dietrich Bonhoeffer put it when he was called out for hanging, 'This is the end, but for me it is the beginning of life.'

Questions

1. What 'everyday suffering' do you experience? How can you find rest in the Lord?
2. What attitude is the Lord challenging regarding the demands people make on you? How can He replace this with Christlikeness?
3. Are you hampered by fear of what God might 'do to you' in order to bring you closer to Him? Look up some verses in your concordance about 'Do not fear.' How can we find our delight in Him, and the fellowship of His suffering, even in our hardest times?

And on that day when my strength is failing
The end draws near and my time has come
Still my tongue will sing your praise unending
Ten thousand years and then forevermore!
Bless the Lord, O my soul, O my soul
Worship His holy name
Sing like never before, O my soul
I'll worship His holy name.
'10,000 Reasons', Matt Redman & Steve Angrisano

10. A Victorious Mother

Julie McAddock

Regardless of the kind of mother you are – adoptive, biological, foster, spiritual – there arc a few things that we all have in common. Joy and fulfilment, I hope, are things we all experience through motherhood. Tiredness and depletion are often the case too! And then there's failure. I don't think I know a mother who doesn't feel on some level like a failure: either a 'recovered' failure, who looks back and wishes she had done things differently, or one who feels she is currently in the process of a daily deep-dive into failure. Or, if you're like me, both.

This isn't the chapter I was expecting to end a book with. I was going about my own business, proofreading an article as part of my freelance work, when I found myself face-to-face with a story that had to be told. Julie McAddock's article hit me right between the eyes, because there is hope for us failures. We can fail BIG, but never bigger than God's love for us.

Julie's story is readily available online. She was frequently drunk and skipping school by the time she hit her teens; before she was twenty, this had escalated to heroin and Valium addictions in addition to alcohol – and she had two young children who were frequently taken into care. The cycle of rehab and relapse, having her children and missing them, felt endless. I asked Julie how the Lord intervened to bring her out of the hopelessness of her early life.

I always knew there was a God. In school we had services every Friday, and we would learn and sing about Him. But He wasn't real or personal to me: 'there is a God,' was my attitude. From time to time, I would pray for help, when I was overwhelmed and wracked with guilt.

And then finally, one day, enough was truly enough. My children were in care, my family weren't talking to me, I had no friends. I was so lonely I didn't want to live. And this time I didn't just pray, I called out to God. 'If you help me, I promise I'll follow you all the days of my life.' I'd never really meant it like that – before, I'd pray, God would help me, and I'd forget all about Him. This time I was determined it would be different, and a woman I'd met two years previously came into my mind – a Christian woman. I called my mother and said 'Mum, before you hang the phone up on me, can you give me her number?'

This lady took me along to a Sunday outreach café. People looked different there, happy. The singing and praising were a bit full on, and at first I felt uncomfortable. But then a man shared his testimony about being freed from chains of addiction. I elbowed the guy next to me: 'That's me! I have those chains!' Then he said those chains were actually his sin.

Now, I'd had lots of labels on me before, but I never knew that my real problem was sin.

I went into a Christian rehab called Teen Challenge in Wales, where I learned truth from the Bible instead of what the world was telling me. I was there for a long time: after a year's programme, I did their leadership training and then worked there for six months. That gave me a good distance from my old life.

When I finally came back to Scotland, I had a sense of pride that I had really made it, and changed – but then the challenges and temptations were huge! When I felt overwhelmed by them, a children's song would come into my mind and remind me who I was now: 'I have decided to follow Jesus; no turning back.' There would be no turning back for me. Even if I slipped up, I didn't allow those mistakes to drag me down – I kept going. I went to meetings and made sure I was accountable to people. When I was really overwhelmed by my thoughts and my past, I would meditate on Proverbs 3:5-6, the verses I'd been given at Teen Challenge:

Even if I slipped up, I didn't allow those mistakes to drag me down – I kept going.

Trust in the Lord with all your heart, and do not lean on your own understanding. In all your ways acknowledge him, and he will make straight your paths.

Being separated from my kids was terrible. I was always sad and full of pain, and they felt the same. We really loved each other. People have a perception that you choose drugs over your children, but it's not like that. You're riddled with guilt and shame.

I am so grateful to have a good relationship with them now. My kids never throw anything in my face. They were just so glad to have their mum back. That doesn't mean we never fall out, but now they know I'm always going to be here. They see what God has done in my life, and I believe He has put healing on them too, even in the ways they don't remember certain things. My daughter wants to be a social worker, and they both really have their heads screwed on!

I believe He has put healing on them too.

When I was in that constant cycle of drinking and shooting up and losing my kids, I felt worse than a failure. I felt like nothing. And when I moved here, I was bombarded by my past. I still felt like that lost, broken person, but God told me I wasn't that girl anymore. I let His truth rule in my life. And I make sure I have time to pray and listen to His voice every day.

God told me I wasn't that girl anymore. I let His truth rule in my life.

I'm not a failure now. I'm a coping and nurturing parent, I have a husband (whom I met in rehab) and two small children with him, and I have a job with responsibilities for my staff. I don't take any of that lightly. I run a charity called Street Connect, a place where women can be restored to God and to their children. It gives them space away from the chaos and help to step down from medication. We see people taking steps forward both from addiction and toward God, but it's generally a pretty rocky road. It can get discouraging when they fall backwards, but you have to keep going with them.[1]

---

1.   Interview on 15/2/22. Find out more at www.streetconnect.co.uk

* * *

He who dwells in the shelter of the Most High will abide in the shadow of the Almighty. I will say to the Lord, 'My refuge and my fortress, my God, in whom I trust.' ... When he calls to me, I will answer him; I will be with him in trouble; I will rescue him and honour him (Ps. 91:1-2, 15).

Have I Failed?

Some of you will read Julie's story and think it's just not for you. Addiction and having your kids taken into care is not the plotline of a typical Christian mum. But here are some things that are:

- Divorce. So clearly, in Scripture, not God's plan for our family life. Yet, sadly, sometimes the place where our broken hearts and relationships lead us.
- Abortion. No, it's not unimaginable to any woman who might pick up this book. It's incredibly common. If you aborted a child and you know that you failed your baby so badly there is no fixing it now, I salute you. You know how big God's grace is, because He saw all that and still lovingly called your name.
- Unsaved kids. You may have tried for decades to win your children for the Lord, and they have made it clear they're sick of it – or they're living in persistent sin and have no wish to repent. They want nothing to do with Him, and you're terrified for their souls.
- Unloving kids. You do your best to pour unselfishly into your children's lives, but they have become offended and

bitterness has taken root. Your relationship is shattered, and it feels like a burden you can't carry for one more day.

- You're totally overwhelmed. Your life and home look like you're thriving, but underneath it you're exhausted, resentful and see only the things you never get done, the goals you haven't met, the events you're missing out on. You act cheerful in public, but inside you feel like you're drowning.

- You are parenting in an un-Christlike way. Whether you can't be bothered meeting up with the woman you're supposed to be mentoring or you can't stop yelling at your kids, you know you aren't living out God's love for them. You ask for forgiveness and help to change, but you fail every single day.

Where is hope?

Don't Give up because you Slipped up

One of the elements in the Bible that gives me great comfort is that it shows the history of God's people, warts and all. The stories of their sin demonstrate the great grace of God to save and use us failures, as well as the perseverance of these same once-sinners who kept messing up but kept getting up. Often, these holy men and women who loved God had to be stopped in their tracks even to see that they had fallen into serious sin. Some of the 'hall of faith' saints in Hebrews 11 are not people we would nominate! And yet, God used their mistakes and rebellion to show us that He still has a plan, despite our mistakes and rebellion.

We spoke in the Mentoring chapter about the need to model repentance before those whom we are parenting or teaching. But first and foremost, our repentance and our encouragement to keep going are aimed toward God. He isn't just the One who covers your sins and mistakes; He is the One who lovingly picks you up and sets you back on the right path. Then walks beside you. Holding your hand. You really can't overstate the willingness of the Saviour to be compassionate with you and present with you at every moment!

In *Gentle and Lowly,* Dane Ortlund writes: 'When you come to Christ for mercy and love and help in your anguish and perplexity and sinfulness, you are going with the flow of his own deepest wishes, not against them...when we hold back, lurking in the shadows, fearful and failing, we miss out not only on our own increased comfort but on Christ's increased comfort. He lives for this. This is what he loves to do. His joy and ours rise and fall together.'[2]

Can you trust Christ to preserve you through all your perceived failures? Or do you keep punishing yourself even after repentance? I love this quotation from Marigold Jones, who felt mired in failure after abandoning her family. She later found the Lord, and with Him hope, and now speaks peace to other mothers who have felt that same despair:

> To the mom who is defined by failure, accept responsibility for your actions and yours alone. **The evils of this world will try to convince you that it is ALL your fault**. The sins of the whole world are not yours to bear. Take your faults and hand

---

2.   Dane Ortlund, *Gentle and Lowly: The Heart of Christ for Sinners and Sufferers.* (Crossway: Wheaton, Illinois, 2020), Chapter 1, 'His Very Heart'

them over to Christ, lest His death is in vain. **He did not die for nothing; He died for your failure**.[3]

Think on what is Good

When my young daughter tells me she can't sleep because she's thinking of scary things, I always tell her the same thing: there's only enough space in your brain for one thing at a time. The way to displace a bad thought is not dwelling on how bad it is and how much you wish you could not think about it – no, it's by replacing it with a good one.

You can't change the past, whether it's five minutes ago or fifty years. You may be able to make amends or repent of old sins, but often the scars remain. If you can't stop dwelling on your failures, you need something else to dwell on. Philippians 4:8 says, '*Finally, brothers, whatever is true, whatever is honorable, whatever is just, whatever is pure, whatever is lovely, whatever is commendable, if there is any excellence, if there is anything worthy of praise, think about these things*.'

> *If you can't stop dwelling on your failures, you need something else to dwell on.*

This is much easier said than done, especially when your brain is on a negative spiral and you feel almost helpless to break out. If you are prone to this – whether it's regrets, temptation, resentment, anxiety, anything – then it's a good idea to prepare ahead for what tools you can use to

---

3.   www.unmaskingthemess.com, 'To the Mother Feeling Like a Failure', March 28, 2017

fill your mind with good things. Cry out to God for help in interrupting these thoughts. Have verses prepared which give you strength, and repeat or read them to yourself as often as you need to. Remember times when Christ lavished His care and provision on You, and give thanks. Sing a hymn to yourself. In these ways, even at my saddest and most anxious, I see the beauty and delight of Jesus Himself and I long to just fall into His arms.

One other thing – a striking point Julie made was her faith that God would lead her children too, and had protected them from harm even before she knew Him. This is a good moment to call to mind what Amy Carmichael observed, that the work with her children belonged to God, not to her; and

If you feel you have failed as a Proverbs 31 woman, concentrate instead on being a 1 Corinthians 13 woman.

Monica's perseverance when it looked like the battle for Christ was hopeless in her son's heart. Why? Because it's too tempting, when we have disappointed our own expectations of our spiritual motherhood, to dwell on the resulting disappointment of how our spiritual children have turned out! Pray for them, of course, but pray in faith that God will act, not with the attitude that you have to fix every problem in your own strength. Unless God builds the house, the worker – and mother – labours in vain! So keep hope, keep faith, and if you feel you have failed as a Proverbs 31 woman, concentrate instead on being a 1 Corinthians 13 woman.

'Bears all things, believes all things, hopes all things, endures all things' (1 Cor. 13:7).

Let His Truth about you Rule

I spoke earlier about a time when, as a young girl, I suffered from an obsessive guilt complex. At that time, I learned to tell myself the truth about how God saw me. I didn't always feel it, but I knew it because the Bible is true. My favourite of these was in 1 John 3:20, *'For whenever our heart condemns us, God is greater than our heart, and he knows everything.'*

I still cling to this verse when I feel confused about whether or not I have made a right decision. The Lord knows my desire is to walk in a right way before Him, and that I do that with all my might. He judges my heart even if I have misjudged my actions, and He sees me as fully justified and one with Him. Samuel Rutherford wrote, 'Believe God's love and power more than you believe your own feelings and experiences. Your rock is Christ, and it is not the rock that ebbs and flows but the sea.'

Believe God's love and power more than you believe your own feelings and experiences.

If you suffer from a lack of assurance of salvation because of sins or past failures, the Sword of the Spirit is your essential weapon for attacking Satan's lies. Colossians 1:22 says, *'he has now reconciled [you] in his body of flesh by his death, in order to present you holy and blameless and above reproach before him.'* This is His will, and nothing can divert God's will. 'Holy and blameless and above reproach' is who you are. Now, even though we are perfectly holy before the Father, Jesus still calls us to change more and more into His likeness, finding greater and greater freedom from sin. And He is going to win this battle too, because He has said so. Paul assures us, *'he who began a good work in you will bring it to completion at the day of Jesus Christ'.*[4] In other words, we are not what we once were, and we are not yet what we will be!

> *'Holy and blameless and above reproach' is who you are.*

What if you have not repented of the ways in which you've let your spiritual children down? Are you inclined toward defensiveness or blaming others for things you know deep-down were your mistakes? Then know that there is freedom to be found. You can be free from all that anger and fear of being exposed. You can be free from resentment and bitterness. You can be free from exhaustion and irritation. All of these are like Julie's addictions – we might slip up, but we will slip up less and less as we learn to handle our urges and temptations. The only defeat is in giving up and letting sin rule. Take the first step: go to Him, lay it all down, and start over. And when the Accuser whispers to you that even Christ Himself is not strong enough to vanquish these sins that keep plaguing you, you just whisper right back: 'That's a lie. Because I heard He will bring His good work to completion in me.'

Press On

I once was a guest on a radio show for Christians, based in the Scottish Highlands. It was exciting to think about my five

---

4.   Philippians 1:6.

all-time favourite Christian songs, and probably my number one is 'Pressing On,' by the slightly unlikely Bob Dylan (if you don't know, he went through an evangelical phase in the 1970s). The song is based on Paul's assertion that '*I press on toward the goal for the prize of the upward call of God in Christ Jesus*' (Phil. 3:14). The song has a driving, urgent beat with a gospel flourish. It's almost onomatapaoeic in the way it repeats 'Pressing on, yes I'm pressing on, I'm pressing on for the higher calling of my Lord.' It's a real keep-you-going kind of tune!

You know, Paul was a good example of pressing on, but Jesus is a better one. He sees everything in our past, He sees sins we've never even noticed in ourselves, and He just persists in loving and forgiving. How many times does He forgive us? Seventy times seven? That sounds about right for me – in an average day! He sees how many times we resist Him, can't be bothered talking to Him, actively rebel against Him, and treat Him ungratefully. But there is only one place in the past that He points us to – and that is His cross.

> *There is only one place in the past that He points us to – and that is His cross.*

Let's go back to that Hall of Faith for a moment. It's filled with the wonderful mothers of old who lived and died before the Lord, made mistakes and pressed on. '*We are surrounded by so great a crowd of witnesses*,' Hebrews 12:1 eloquently encourages us. I've always misinterpreted this verse to mean there was a sort of cheering crowd on the bleachers of my life, but that is placing a wrong emphasis on the words 'witnesses'.

The saints of old are not witnessing, or observing us – they are witnessing to Christ and His finished work.

Throughout Hebrews 11, we are encouraged to follow the example of Old Testament. Verse 39 tells us that they have all become witnesses through faith, but never received the fulfilment of God's promises. They were part of the story, but we are all being perfected together as one body. We are all witnesses together, running the same race, just at different times. And what is the ultimate motivation of this race? *'Looking unto Jesus, the author and finisher of our faith; who for the joy that was set before him endured the cross, despising the shame, and is set down at the right hand of the throne of God'* (Heb. 12:2).

Press on because He pressed on. Press on because He is now pressing on, on your behalf, 'sitting at the right hand of the throne of God.' Just as in this book, the generations who have gone before us can give us practical tutorials on what pressing on might look like, but what is the ultimate answer for every struggle in our Christian life? I know I keep repeating it, but that's because I myself have to constantly keep learning it! **Look at Jesus.**

He is now pressing on, on your behalf, 'sitting at the right hand of the throne of God.'

Where do we see Jesus Fail?

You may think Jesus has nothing to do with failure. And you're right in that, in the grand scheme of God's plan, He is the ultimate victor. But there is one sense in which He almost constantly failed – people's expectations of Him. That's one thing we haven't talked about, but it's one of the most powerful ways in which we feel defeat. If you feel guilty or burdened, it can be an illuminating exercise to work out whether your guilt is aimed toward God (repentance) or toward people (fear of man). As we discussed earlier, Jesus had an audience of One – so He didn't let Himself be dragged off course or mired by the feeling He had let everyone down. In fact, it's precisely by following His Father, not His earthly friends or family, that He disappointed people's expectations the most:

- He failed to meet His parents' understanding of what His childhood duty looked like.
- He failed to condone or even stay silent on the hypocrisy and spiritual abuse of the Jewish ruling elders.
- He failed to deliver Israel from the occupying Roman empire.
- He failed to act as His own disciples thought a King should!
- He failed to condemn or punish those that His followers considered their enemies.
- He failed to judge those that other people considered dirty or immoral, as they projected their own 'offended' opinions onto God.
- He failed to bring the Jews the kingdom of renewed riches, power and earthly authority they were expecting.
- He failed to dilute His message for Pilate's benefit, and therefore suffered the 'failure' of death.

Jesus was relentlessly persecuted for failing to conform to other people's desires, and if the same happens to you when you really have done your utmost to serve God and others well, know that you are sharing in His sufferings. Look at how He dealt with people in that situation: He remained kind and open toward them, but was rock-solid in His example that His identity, attitudes and service were all rooted in His Father and He could not be shaken by anyone else's opinions of Him.

People will try to make you feel bad for failing their expectations. They may try to lay failure on you for accomplishing less than they hoped; for refusing to condone or enable their own sin; for saying 'no' at times when you're unable to commit to a task or ministry; for all kinds of ways in which you won't meet their standards. And that is not your problem. Keep your eyes fixed. Press on.

Verses on Overcoming Failure

Therefore lift your drooping hands and strengthen your weak knees, and make straight paths for your feet, so that what is lame may not be put out of joint but rather be healed (Heb. 12:12, quoting Isa. 35:3).

In both Hebrews and Isaiah, the context is that of God's people undergoing discipline. They've been in a hard, weary, discouraging place. You know that feeling when you're just dragging yourself through life, striving and almost in despair? We're not called to live in that place. And that's good news! Stand straight. Walk easy. How? How can you do this when you feel bent double by failure and worry? Next verse please ...

Stand straight.
Walk easy.

This is the confidence we have in approaching God: that if we ask anything according to his will, he hears us. And if we know that he hears us – whatever we ask – we know that we have what we asked of him (1 John 5:14-15 NIV).

Now, we equivocate on this verse. Of course, we believe He *can* do all things – we just don't believe He *will*. And here's what I would say, and my challenge to myself. Live as if you have perfect confidence that God is already in the process of answering your prayers. It's true that sometimes He answers in a way we don't expect. Sometimes He makes us wait in order to build something new in us, or work in a different arena. But if you can trust completely that the things you ask for His sake will be given, that He has a plan already underway which is better even than you asked or imagined, then you can stand straight and walk easy. His answers do not depend on the quantity or quality of our faith, but if we ask believing that He will answer, we can live with peace and we can be prepared to follow His leading as He uses us along the way.

> *Live as if you have perfect confidence that God is already in the process of answering your prayers.*

And if the weight on your heart is primarily focused on the past, know that that prayer has already been answered. You are completely forgiven of all repented sin. You are free. The Father looks at you in His perfect holiness, and He sees it reflected back at Him. You are not a failure.

When my soul was embittered, when I was pricked in heart, I was brutish and ignorant; I was like a beast toward you. Nevertheless, I am continually with you; you hold my right hand. You guide me with your counsel, and afterward you will receive me to glory (Ps. 73:21-24).

When you were getting it wrong, when you felt alone, when your prayers seemed to bounce off the ceiling, when you couldn't see out of the deep hole you were in, know this: God never gave up on you. You have awakened to His touch on your hand; you can now walk in His guidance and counsel, and You can know all the joy of anticipating His perfect presence and delight.

Questions

1. How do you feel you have failed as a spiritual mother and a spiritual woman?
2. What are some specific Scriptures, thanks and hymns which would help you to reorient your negative thoughts in line with Philippians 4:8?
3. What are ways in which you would like to do better in the future? How can Christ's example and your identity in Him help you do this?

> *There's power in the mighty name of Jesus*
> *Every war He wages He will win*
> *I'm not backing down from any giant*
> *'Cause I know how this story ends.*
>
> *Yes, I know how this story ends*
> *I'm gonna see a victory, I'm gonna see a victory*
> *For the battle belongs to You, Lord.*
> – 'See a Victory', Elevation Worship

Acknowledgements and Epilogue

This book is an end-product of the many mothers who have blessed me with their care, their prayers and their example. My own mother has been sacrificial in her love for as long as I can remember – and it may yet be that, like the Lord, 'to grey hairs she will carry me'! And I am grateful not only for her, but for Ruby Patrick, the woman who first modelled Christian womanhood to my mother, and is thus also a part of my chain. Ruby is now enjoying her reward in heaven, but her work for the Lord Jesus lives on in the legacy of my family.

My mother-in-law, Catriona, is a picture of gracious perseverance and selfless provision, as well as a wonderful friend. Bonnie Dusenbury prays for me daily and shares her heart with me in joy and in sorrow, a truly faithful woman. Rachel Nixon, my 'smallest' big sister, is one of my all-round heroes and I still try to follow her example of cheerfulness, generosity and fortitude. Catriona Lamont is the complete picture of the Proverbs 31 woman, tireless in her work for the Lord and her love for those He has placed in her care. Louise

MacMillan, Irene Howat, Anne Norrie (also my wonderful proof editor) and Christine Stone are all women who 'see' me and have nurtured me in different ways. I suppose if I go on much longer I'll have to thank the Academy as well – there is not space enough to mention all my teachers, encouragers and examples from thirty-eight years of Christian womanhood!

I am very grateful to the team at Christian Focus, especially my editor, Rosanna Burton, who keeps me going, answers my questions patiently, and saves me from total writing solitude as she helps me shape the book and Colin Fast, who is carrying on her good work!

Thank you to Rabbi Cosmo Panzetta, who, when I confessed that I was riffing off his Bible teaching yet again, assured me that we are all messengers giving the same truths from the Lord. Cosmo has been one of the great spiritual influences of my life, persistently calling me to conform my heart to Christ's, and I can't recommend his daily Bible teaching enough to anyone who wants a 'new beginning' in their Christian walk.

Finally, enormous thanks to all those who contributed to this book or let me pick their brains: Sharon Dickens, Shanana Beattie, Emily Colson, Lisa Harper, Sara Gordon, and Carlee Nicholson. I am grateful to the Lord who led me to each one of you. You have blessed me and I hope this book blesses you.

When I was telling my friend Shanana about the concept of this book, she said, 'Please write about my friend Joan. She has welcomed so many of us students who came from far away to her church and stayed. She has cooked for us, and taught us to cook. She's had us in her home. She's advised us and comforted us. I can give you so many names of people who will tell you the impact she's had on their lives. Please – if you don't tell her story, no one will, and one day it will be forgotten.'

I objected: 'But there are no books written about Joan. No further resources I can direct people to.'

'The resources,' Shanana said, 'are the *Joans* in their own lives.'

I can't argue with that. I didn't end up using Joan as a full chapter, but I can't think of a better way to end this book on spiritual motherhood than by pointing to this beautiful testimony from a spiritual child. Joan's work may not live on in a detailed memorial, but it will in the fruit of all those she has taken in and mentored and blessed.

Learn all you can from the Joans in your own life. And, as you grow in your own faith and maturity before the Lord, go and do likewise.

Resources and Further Reading

Here, I'd like to tell you a little more about the books and resources I used in compiling this compendium of wonderful spiritual mothers. Happily, many of them are free! To switch things up a little, though, I'm going to categorise them according to how you may find them most useful.

Biographical works

Murray, Iain, *Amy Carmichael: Beauty for Ashes*, (Banner of Truth: Edinburgh, 2015). An excellent brief summary of a life that every Christian should know.

Severance, Diana Lynn, *Feminine Threads: Women in the Tapestry of Christian History*. (Christian Focus: Fearn, 2011). A brilliantly analysed overview of women both celebrated and unknown through the whole history of the Church.

On the Happy Life: St Augustine's Cassiciacum Dialogues, volume 2. Michael P. Foley, ed., (Yale University Press: New Haven & London,

2019). While not light reading, this classical dialogue between Augustine, his friends, his son and his mother offer an interesting glimpse into an 'entertainment' for the tightly knit group in the brief period between Augustine's conversion and Monica's death. The notes and exposition are particularly helpful.

https://quod.lib.umich.edu/e/evans
N07808.0001.001/1:13?rgn=div1;view=fulltext
A free and fascinating account of early American Christianity, including informal glimpses of Jonathan and Sarah Edwards' home life.

https://newwhitchurch.press/parr/lamentation. A free digital copy of Katherine Parr's best-known Christian work. Beautifully written and searingly honest, you will feel you know her after reading her meditations.

Prentiss, George, *The Life and Letters of Elizabeth Prentiss*. This work is public domain. The copy I cited was downloaded on Apple Books (sadly, there is no publisher's info – mine had a green cover image!), but you can access a free copy on Gutenberg:
https://www.gutenberg.org/ebooks/11549
This book moves slowly but with great beauty, and here you will meet a funny, tender, godly friend.

Devotional resources for spiritual mothers
Harper, Lisa, *The Sacrament of Happy: What a Smiling God Brings to a Wounded World*, (B &H Publishing Group: Nashville, 2017). An uplifting and relatable account of the struggle to find joy, regardless of circumstances.

Carmichael, Amy, *Candles in the Darkness*. (Triangle: 1981). A collection of excerpts from Amy's letters, containing beautiful truths and heartrending challenges.

Colson, Emily, *Dancing with Max: A Mother and Son who Broke Free*, (Zondervan: Grand Rapids, 2010). Albeit this is an autobiographical work, I place it here because it will minister to any woman who is nurturing a child or young believer. Its lessons are too many to expound here – just read it.

Ortlund, Dane, *Gentle and Lowly: The Heart of Christ for Sinners and Sufferers.* (Crossway: 2020). A deeply comforting meditation on our Lord's character and heart for us.

www.unmaskingthemess.com.
A place to go to see that you are not alone in the struggle, and be pointed back to Jesus.

https://www.youtube.com/c/HouseofNewBeginnings
A treasure trove of excellent teaching from my American minister, Messianic rabbi Cosmo Panzetta.

Resources for mentoring and mothering other Christians
https://20schemes.com
While 20schemes is a church-planting organisation working in deprived communities, their articles and resources are excellent. Join the women's email list to receive the 17 Questions for mentoring – an invaluable tool for spiritual accountability.

Sharon Dickens, *Unconventional*, 10Publishing, forthcoming. I recommend any of Sharon's books, though this one gets down to nitty-gritty detail on the how and why of women's ministries. Her writing is always incisive, down-to-earth and inspiring to 'go and do likewise.'

https://www.streetconnect.co.uk
Julie McAddock's charity for women overcoming addiction issues while working through their relationship with their children is a great place to go if you are dealing with complicated layers in a mentee. It also includes resources and more about Julie's story.

Resources for mentoring and mothering children and teenagers
Lloyd-Jones, Sally. *The Jesus Storybook Bible*. Zondervan: 2012. This book is so sympathetically written and so Christ-focussed that I have not only read it through with my children (many times, for some chapters) but have even bought it for adults.

Tripp, Paul. *Age of Opportunity: A Biblical Guide for Parenting Teens*. P&R, 2001. Honestly, I may as well put all of Paul Tripp's books here, because I've found them incredibly heart-challenging and counter-cultural since first reading *Instruments in the Redeemer's Hands* years ago. This one is also appropriate for parenting small children, despite the subtitle.
Chapter 2 of Age of Opportunity can be accessed free online: https://assets.speakcdn.com/assets/1804/excerpt_age_of_opportunity.pdf